Collins

Presentation Skills

IN

7

SIMPLE STEPS

WITHDRAWN

Collins

HarperCollins Publishers
77-85 Fulham Palace Road
Hammersmith
London W6 8JB

First edition 2014
Reprint 10 9 8 7 6 5 4 3 2 1 0
© HarperCollins Publishers 2014
ISBN 978-0-00-750719-1
Collins ® is a registered trademark of HarperCollins Publishers Limited.
www.collinselt.com
A catalogue record for this book is available from the British Library
Typeset in India by Aptara
Printed and bound in Great Britain by Clays Ltd, St Ives plc

HarperCollins does not warrant that www.collinselt.com or any other website
mentioned in this title will be provided uninterrupted, that any website will be error
free, that defects will be corrected, or that the website or the server that makes it
available are free of viruses or bugs. For full terms and conditions please refer to the
site terms provided on the website.

Every effort has been made to contact the holders of copyright material, but if any have
been inadvertently overlooked, the Publisher will be pleased to make the necessary
arrangements at the first opportunity.

Illustrations by Scott Garrett

MIX
Paper from
responsible sources
FSC C007454
www.fsc.org

FSC™ is a non-profit international organisation established to promote the
responsible management of the world's forests. Products carrying the FSC
label are independently certified to assure consumers that they come from
forests that are managed to meet the social, economic and ecological needs
of present and future generations, and other controlled sources.

Find out more about HarperCollins and the environment at
www.harpercollins.co.uk/green

Contents

About the author

James Schofield has worked for various multinational companies and governmental departments in Asia and Europe for more than twenty-five years. He is employed by a large electronics company as a business coach and management trainer with a focus on creativity and communication, and in particular, presentation skills. James has presented to audiences from 1–500+ around the world and has experienced and learnt how to handle the challenges that giving a presentation can throw at you.

PREPARE FOR ANYTHING AND EVERYTHING

'The person who uses a lot of big words is not trying to inform you; he's trying to impress you.'
— Oskar von Miller, engineer (1855–1934)

Five ways to succeed

- Start small – contribute actively in meetings.
- Look for opportunities to give presentations.
- Get tips in advance from experienced presenters.
- Take risks – try out different approaches to presentations.
- Ask for feedback and learn from your mistakes.

Five ways to fail

- Avoid presentation opportunities.
- Leave preparations to the last minute.
- Prepare everything alone.
- Be overconfident.
- Assume your audience shares your opinion.

Getting motivated

So, a couple of weeks ago your boss asked you to give a presentation but now, as the deadline gets closer, you're having doubts. What made you say yes? The first thing to realise is that you're not alone, and this book is about the difference between those for whom presentations will always be a form of medieval torture and those who learn to enjoy them. Because learning how to present is a really good idea.

Profile

There are many ways to get yourself noticed at work. Some, like singing *My Way* on a karaoke machine at the office party, won't help your career. Others, like being good at your job, probably will. But combining being good at your job with the ability to stand in front of a bunch of strangers or your colleagues and tell them about it will get you to the top.

Transferable life skills

Presentation skills have a wide application. You'll be able to talk with confidence and assurance to complete strangers. You'll be able to get people to listen to you and you'll be able to use your voice and body language to influence people. These skills are useful at work and outside it as well. Think about the possibilities.

Knowledge sharing

This is the information age. But it can be difficult to sort out the relevant information from what is irrelevant. When you give a presentation, you'll find that you attract people to you who can add information to what you know already and make it better. It's a simple calculation: talk to one colleague about what you're doing and you'll get one person's input, which may or may not be useful. Talk to fifty and the chances are much higher that you'll learn something new that you can use.

Networking

Presenting will give you great opportunities to network with a lot of like-minded people at the same time. Who knows, one of them might be the person who gives you your dream job at some time in the future.

Fixing the parameters

Before you start work on your presentation, it's smart to do some research. The more you find out about what's required in advance, the better the end result.

Presentation types

The first thing you need to find out is what kind of presentation is required. There are several types, each with its own distinct purpose and challenges.

1 Information sharing

This is the most frequent type of presentation. It's used for bringing a group of people up to speed about a topic of mutual relevance, for example sharing information about the status of a project or changes in the organisation. Sometimes you might be asked to present regularly at a monthly meeting. It's important for information-sharing presentations to sound neutral because people need to be allowed to draw their own conclusions about what you tell them. If you don't sound neutral, then you run the risk that your audience will reject what you say because they believe you to be biased. So the challenge lies in sounding neutral without being dull. You can do this by making clear to people how something affects them directly: *As soon as the system is ready, we need to be able to use it efficiently*.

2 Training

Although a lot of companies now use fewer classroom training sessions, there are still many situations where they are the best way to share knowledge quickly. If you are the expert for a particular system, process or tool, you may be asked to train other users even if you don't have a background in training.

The difficulty is to judge how quickly your audience will get the key points. What might seem dead easy to you could be baffling to them. On the other hand, if you make things too easy, you run the risk of your audience feeling patronised. A good approach is to collect feedback as you go. This could take the form of asking 'test' questions after each central point: *So, those are the advantages I see with the new software. How do you feel about them?* This helps you to gauge if you're getting the content level right for your audience.

3 Selling

For some people 'selling' is still a dirty word. It smacks of pushy door-to-door sales people or TV shopping channels. But actually, we all need to sell things, even if it's our own skills, when we go for a job interview.

The key to being good at sales is to think how your product or service will make the life of the listener better: *Using this database is going to make your research much more accurate.* If you approach sales with this attitude, you can feel comfortable with what you are doing.

4 Introducing change

It's a fact that most people don't like change. We're all creatures of habit so when we first hear about something new, we tend to reject it as unnecessary. There is often an element of fear in this response. A change can have an impact on people's own interests, aspects of their jobs and even their personality, and as a result, an audience may have very negative reactions to the presenter. Everyone who tries to introduce change experiences this, from a top CEO trying to restructure her entire company down to a team assistant who wants to convince his office colleagues that a new rota system for making coffee in the morning is mission critical.

What can you do to combat this? The best way is to get the people affected involved in discussion. Simply informing them of a change is likely to lead to resistance, either active *(Who do you think you are? I'm not doing that!)* or passive *(I'll get round to doing that – sometime)*. So outline to the audience what the current situation is, give clear reasons why change is necessary, outline possible solutions, and then engage the audience in discussion about the merits or demerits of these solutions. Let the audience see that you are interested in their opinions and want to involve them in finding the best solution. That way you'll get them on board and willing to cooperate.

Clarifying objectives

Once you've worked out what kind of presentation is needed, you can move on to thinking about what you need to achieve. To do this, you need to answer four key questions.

■ How much time have you got?

■ What practical details should you check about the audience?

■ What influence does their part of the company have on them?

■ What is your goal in the time available?

1 How much time have you got?

This is a question that needs to be clarified with the presentation organisers before you start detailed preparation. It's important because if you don't know how much time you have, it's easy to produce too much material for the time you have available. There are several possible consequences.

■ You're asked to stop before you get to the conclusion.

■ You rush through your material and lose your audience because they can't keep up with you.

■ You don't have enough time to deal with questions from your audience.

It's hard to define how much time you should allow for questions and discussions because it depends on how controversial the topic is and the type of presentation you're giving. But in general, it's advisable to plan for at least twenty-five per cent of your time slot to be given over to dealing with questions.

2 What practical details should you check about the audience?

Your audience should always be in the foreground of your preparation. Ask yourself these questions.

■ *How many people will be there?* The number will have an impact on what technology you use and how you talk to them. If it's only a small number, you can ask them direct questions or get them to discuss something. With a larger audience, you might need a microphone and speakers.

■ *What do they know about my topic already?* Don't overestimate their knowledge or underestimate their intelligence. If it's a complex topic, use a simple analogy that they can relate to. For example, you could compare an electrical circuit with traffic flow controlled by traffic lights. If you're giving an internal presentation, think about what your colleagues already know and what will be new to them.

■ *How do they feel about my topic?* The reaction of your audience can normally be predicted. Be ready for this by preparing concrete evidence to confirm what you're saying.

■ *What can they do with the information they get from me?* Ideally, you should give your audience something they can take away and use themselves. On the other hand, in a regular internal meeting you may need to get information from some of your colleagues. Make sure you get it.

Take this pro-active approach to your presentation and it will come through in the way that you talk about your subject. If you treat an audience as you would a friend, they'll return the favour.

3 What influence does their part of the company have on them?

Finding out where your audience comes from can be enormously important because you might need to adapt your message or style depending on their background. Supposing you had to present a recommendation to introduce new accounting software to different groups within a company, how might you need to change the focus of your talk? What things should you take into account?

■ Management will want to hear about the cost savings that it will generate. The technical side will likely be unimportant to them except for any risks caused by technical problems.

■ IT will want to be reassured by your description of its development that it fits into what they already have. They will be concerned about any difficulties that the new software may cause their servers.

■ Accounting staff will want to know if the software will make their work more accurate.

■ Sales people will expect you to sell something to them so they will be less interested in the development of the product and more interested in how it will make their lives easier.

This is just the beginning; you might need to present the topic to people who have just joined the company or students from a local business college. And of course, you might well have representatives from all these different groups in your audience. The point is, the more you know about their interests, the better able you are to tailor the presentation to them.

4 What's your goal?

There's an old saying: *If you don't know where you're going, you'll never get there.* It's essential to have a clear idea of what you want and what's possible in the time available. Better to aim low and hit your target than be too ambitious and miss completely; so write down a sentence defining your goal: *After my presentation, management can make a decision about whether or not to implement the proposed software.*

Now test your goal to see whether it's realistic by applying the **SMART** (**S**pecific, **M**easurable, **A**ttainable, **R**elevant, **T**imed) criteria to it. In the example above, the goal is:

- ■ Specific (decision on the software)

- ■ Measurable (a decision will be made)

- ■ Attainable (management can make the decision based on your information)

- ■ Relevant (a decision needs to be made)

- ■ Timed (after your presentation).

14

Getting help

Once you've sorted out the parameters for your presentation, it's time to look around for people or tools that can help you to get ready. Since you're reading this book, you've already taken the first step in that direction – congratulations! But there are other things you can do to stack the odds in your favour.

Finding a mentor

Most people are willing to share their experience with less experienced presenters. Look for somebody who could act as a presentation mentor. It could be somebody you've seen giving a good presentation or it could be a co-worker whom you trust. Ask them to observe you doing a dry run of your presentation and to give you feedback. If possible, film it and watch it yourself to learn what can be improved.

Learning from the internet

The internet is full of information on every aspect of presentations, whether it's the creation of visual aids or people giving live presentations. Some of these can be confusing rather than helpful but the TED Talks (www.ted.com) are a good source of excellent presentations to watch . These short talks (3–20 minutes) are entertaining, interesting and some of the best real-life models of what you want to achieve.

Collecting your material

Once you have these supporting elements in place, you can start getting together the material you need for your presentation. What should you be aware of?

Staying relevant

It sounds obvious but the most important thing to remember about your choice of material is that it must be relevant. All of it. There's always a temptation to include an unnecessary story or visual aid because it's entertaining or interesting. Shoot these puppies right at the start of your preparation because if you allow them into your presentation, you will quickly get fond of them and they'll be much harder to get rid of later when you realise you have a time problem. Everything you include must underpin the presentation goal that you set yourself before you get to this stage.

Quality

Again, this may sound obvious but are you sure that the information you're presenting is correct? Have you considered points of view other than your own? Do your conclusions make sense? If you're presenting a topic to a group of experts from your own field, you can guarantee that they'll spot any inaccuracies in your claims. Make sure you can justify anything that you say.

Quantity

There is an important reason why you need to be careful about quantity – your audience's capacity to absorb what you have to say. We find it hard to remember the content of a presentation if there are too many distinct points in it. This means that ideally you should limit what you say to three main points. This isn't always possible, but it's very hard for your audience to process and retain more than four points.

So what do you do if you look at the material you've collected and you feel that your presentation needs more than just three points to get the desired concept across? You have to cluster your information into three to four key headings. Look at this example.

Subject: New software
Key points: faster processing of information, handles larger quantities of data, support from external consultants necessary, high costs of new licences, hardware update necessary to handle new software, staff training necessary for new software, complex company-wide rollout, better data security

These eight key points can be clustered under three distinct headings. For example:

■ **New software advantages:** faster processing of information, handles larger quantities of data, better data security

■ **New software disadvantages:** high costs of new licences, staff training necessary for new software, complex company-wide rollout

■ **Recommendation:** support from external consultants necessary, hardware update necessary

Your audience will remember the three headings from your presentation and if they want the details, they can check the handouts or a copy of the presentation that you can make available for them.

Processing your material

Once you've collected your material and clustered it under three main headings, you need to reduce each point under those headings into the essential information that you must be got across. For each point, create 'must know' statements and then turn each statement into key words. These key words will be very helpful later when you're creating your presentation notes and your visual aids so it's worth investing the time. Here are some examples.

■ **New software advantages**

Must know: *The data can be handled much faster by the new software.*

Key words: Faster data processing

Must know: *The new software will increase the degree of data security.*

Key words: Data security increased

■ **New software disadvantages**

Must know: *Staff will need to be trained on the new system.*

Key words: Staff training necessary

Must know: *The new software licences are expensive.*

Key words: Cost of new licences

■ **Recommendation**

Must know: *For the complex company-wide rollout, we'll need external consultants.*

Key words: External consultants for rollout

This processing of your material is just as necessary for diagrams and charts. Always look at them with a critical eye and ask yourself how you can cut, reduce and simplify them so that the point you're trying to make is as clear as possible.

Developing an appropriate style

Later on we're going to look in detail at how to give your presentation real impact, but it's worth considering what can make you a stylish presenter from the very start.

Being clear

If you talk to your audience in language that they can relate to, then you're treating them with a respect that they will return. But giving a presentation can sometimes bring about alarming changes in a speaker. Firstly, there are speakers who litter their presentation with obscure acronyms such as SOD (separation of duties) or SOX (Sarbanes Oxley Act) that are common in their field but not known outside it. Secondly, there are speakers who have the mistaken belief that they need to use a particular style of business jargon in order to be taken seriously by their audience. Presenters no longer look for ways to work together, they look for 'synergies'. They don't encourage staff, they 'incentivise' them. They don't have detailed plans, they have plans with a 'high degree of granularity'.

The effect of this business gobbledygook is to set up a barrier between the speaker and the audience. When that happens, the audience switches off mentally and starts waiting for the talk to finish.

Appearance

It's unfair but we make judgments about people when we first meet them so you should try to wear clothes that meet your audience's expectations. This doesn't always mean you have to wear a business suit; if you're talking to a group of software programmers, they may not take you seriously looking like that. Before your presentation, check what audience you can expect and dress slightly more formally than them, while remaining comfortable. Uncomfortable clothes can be distracting; avoid wearing a collar that's too tight or shoes that have too high a heel even if you look great in them. That way you can devote all your attention to the job at hand. And always remember: what might look stunning in the mirror at home can seem very skimpy when you're standing in front of a room full of people and all eyes are on you.

Irritators

Doesn't it drive you mad when somebody you are talking to seems to feel the need to tell you what you should and shouldn't do? When we're presenting, we need to be careful that we don't turn people off our message by using what linguists call *irritators*. But what are typical irritators and how can you avoid them?

1 *we/our* vs. *you/your*

Very often in a presentation you're making recommendations for some kind of change. Using *we* instead of *you* increases the feeling that everybody is involved. If you use *you*, it can sound as if you're blaming your audience for something they've done wrong. Compare these examples.

■ *You need to introduce the new software quickly.* (Subtext: Why didn't you do it before? I would have.)

We need to introduce the new software. (Neutral statement of fact.)

■ *Your systems have security weaknesses.* (Subtext: Obviously a careless team.)

Our systems have security weaknesses. (We all have a problem.)

2 *must* vs. *have to*

The difference between *must* and *have to* is slight but it can be important. Use *must* when you're talking about something that you want to do because it's important to you: *We must finish the report by Friday* (because we need it for something).

Avoid using *have to* unless you're talking about an external power that is compelling you to do something: *We have to finish the report by Friday* (because otherwise we're in trouble).

3 *Yes, and … / Yes. However, … / No, because … vs. Yes, but …*

Why is it that when we disagree with something, we often say *Yes, but …*, which we all know means *No*? Is it because we don't want to offend the person we're talking to? Whatever the reason, it's dishonest and it can be annoying for your audience. But what do you do when somebody asks a question and it's plain they've missed your message? For example: *Why do the staff need extra training with the new software? It's just an upgrade of the previous version. Surely they can just learn it on their own, can't they?*

Here are some ways of answering a question like that without alienating the listener.

■ Listen to the question and add a reason to back up your argument: *Yes, and if we also provide some training, we can make sure they use all the new features of the upgrade now rather than later.*

■ Listen to the question and politely contradict with a reason: *Yes. However, if we provide some training, we can make sure they use all the new features of the upgrade now rather than later.*

■ Contradict with an honest answer: *No, because unless we provide some training, they won't use all the new features of the upgrade straight away.*

You should be careful with the last version and only use it when you are confident of your audience. However, it's a real answer and so is preferable to *Yes, but …*.

Presentation friendliness

Can the material be put across easily in the time you're allowed? It doesn't make any sense t > include material that's too complex and unwieldy. Sometimes it might be necessary to compromise and provide the audience with a handout or a link where they can get the relevant information after your talk if they're interested, rather than try to show or explain something that's unsuitable for the presentation medium. For example, trying to show lines of computer code to an audience – even if they are fanatical programmers – is going to send most of them to sleep. It's much better to demonstrate what the code can do and tell those people who are interested that you will show them the code personally after the presentation.

Attitude

Finally, whether you enjoy giving a presentation is largely down to your attitude. If you think it's going to be awful, you'll probably be proved right. If you think it's going to be great, the presentation will probably be great too. So you need to go into the presentation with the feeling that it's a conversation with friends. Your audience might be people you don't know yet but they're going to be friends after you've finished because you've got something to tell them that excites you, and you've put in the preparation time so it'll excite them too.

Remember: you are in charge. You've been asked to present. The result is in your hands, nobody else's. Show them what you can do!

Key take-aways

Think about the things you will take away from Step 1 and how you will implement them.

Topic	Take-away	Implementation
How to get motivated about giving a presentation	• *Giving presentations can benefit my career.*	• *I'll look for an opportunity in the near future.*
Deciding what type of presentation is needed		
How to analyse my audience in advance and use this information to improve my presentation		
How to make sure the presentation has a realistic goal		
How to get help		
How to prepare the presentation material		
How to talk		
How to look		
How to give a good impression		

Step 2

CHOOSE YOUR TOOLS AND STRUCTURE

'The best way of learning anything is by doing.'
— Richard Branson,
businessman and entrepreneur

Five ways to succeed

■ Think what your audience wants from your presentation.

■ Give your presentation a clear structure.

■ Take time to prepare your visual method.

■ Get feedback from friends and colleagues in advance.

■ Do a dry run of your presentation.

Five ways to fail

■ Use lots of acronyms.

■ Cover your slides with too much text.

■ Assume your audience knows a lot about your topic.

■ Patronise your audience.

■ Talk for longer than you are scheduled for.

Presentation structure

You can improve your chances of giving a successful presentation by paying attention to its structure. There are many ways to construct a presentation but here are three approaches that can be effectively used for most situations.

The Classical approach

This is based on the idea that the best way to get a message across is to repeat it. Our brains sometimes need time to adjust to a new concept and this method allows the audience to familiarise themselves with it. Here's how it works.

1 Tell 'em what you're going to say

In the introduction, after saying who you are and what your subject is, outline the main points you want to talk about.

2 Tell 'em

In the main body of the presentation, clearly outline each of your main points, making sure that you provide supporting evidence for each of your ideas. Use signposting language (see Step 4) so that your audience can see that you have finished one topic and have moved on to the next. That will help to retain their attention.

3 Tell 'em what you said

At the end, give your audience a summary of the key points of your presentation and what you want them to do with this information.

The FAB approach

The **FAB** (Features, Advantages, Benefits) approach appeals to the heart as well as the mind of the audience and is particularly powerful if you're presenting a product or service. Here's how it works.

1 Features

Explain the features of the product or service: *This camera can send high-resolution pictures instantly to any email address.*

2 Advantages

Show what makes this different from other products or services: *It's no longer necessary to download the pictures onto a computer.*

3 Benefits

Make clear how this improves the life of the user: *With this camera, you can be the first to get the pictures for a breaking story.*

Ultimately, most of our purchasing decisions are based on an emotional response to stimulus but we need to justify our decision with logic or else we feel we've been manipulated. This is what **FAB** can help the presenter to do.

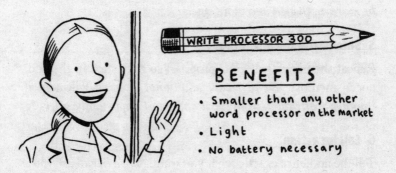

WRITE PROCESSOR 300

BENEFITS
- Smaller than any other word processor on the market
- Light
- No battery necessary

The Persuasive approach

If you've done your research properly, you might realise that there will be people in your audience who are sceptical about your arguments. The Persuasive approach can help you to predict what their objections are likely to be and eliminate them before they start asking questions. Here's how it works.

1 Give your proposed solution

Explain what you want: *We need to provide more technical training to our sales team before they meet with customers.*

2 Go through the disadvantages of the solution

Show the audience that you are aware of possible problems with your solution: *Of course, this means some initial additional costs.*

3 Destroy the disadvantages

Point out why the objections are redundant: *However, making the sales team more effective will result in an increase in sales that will compensate for the costs of training.*

4 Go through the advantages

Now start to sell your proposal: *A better trained sales team will be more motivated and more efficient.*

5 Summarise the advantages

Repeat the benefits of your proposal so they stick in the audience's memory: *So to recap, additional training will actually improve motivation, team spirit and, most importantly, sales.*

6 Call for action

Tell the audience exactly what you want: *So, I'd like to ask you to approve the budget for additional training for our team.*

Choosing presentation tools

Unless you have to stand up and talk without any visual aids, you'll want to make your key points visible to your audience. Here are three possibilities with their own pros and cons.

Microsoft PowerPoint

PowerPoint is the most commonly used presentation tool.

Pros:

■ It's a powerful tool that allows you to organise your information into slides. These can be projected onto a screen with a multimedia projector, enabling large groups of people to see your presentation. You can use text, pictures, films and sounds, and vary the parameters so that each presentation appears unique.

■ It's installed on most business computers so you shouldn't have a problem showing it on any computer.

■ It is the standard software of a professional person.

Cons:

■ Your message can seem boring, especially when you're presenting something that is innovative and creative.

■ You can drown your message under the bells and whistles available in PowerPoint. Just because you *can* add the sound of machine gun fire as your bullet points appear on the screen, doesn't mean you should. Your audience may become confused or more interested in the presentation technology than your message.

Prezi

Prezi (see www.prezi.com) is an interesting alternative to PowerPoint. It takes a different approach to presentations, which can be very stimulating. Essentially, you have a blank screen onto which you can stick text, pictures or other media, which allows you to build up an electronic collage or map. Once you have collected your material, you tell the program the sequence it should follow through your presentation.

Pros:

- The presentation moves in and out of the material you want to show, giving the audience a more dynamic and involving experience of your topic.

- Unlike PowerPoint, there are no pre-set templates so you have a vast amount of freedom to decide what things should look like.

- Prezi is cloud-based, which means the software is hosted on the company's server and you don't have to download any software onto your computer. It also means several people can work on different parts of the presentation at the same time.

Cons:

- The approach can be off-putting and confusing to an audience familiar with PowerPoint. As you move from one point to the next, the text and images zoom in and out and spin around so you can end up feeling as if you're on a ride in a funfair.

All in all, Prezi works best for presentations where you want to show a lot of pictures rather than text.

Flipcharts

Flipcharts are large sheets of paper prepared in advance of a presentation. Generally, they are colourful and eye-catching.

Pros:

■ Your audience will be surprised to see you steering clear of PowerPoint and this will encourage them to pay closer attention to what you have to say.

■ Flipcharts are technology light. If there's somewhere to hang your flipcharts, you don't need to worry about equipment malfunctions.

Cons:

■ Flips need time and some artistic talent to prepare.

■ Flips are not always as easily adaptable as computer-based presentations.

■ Flips work best in small groups of not more than 20 people.

Flips are best for informal workshops or training sessions.

Introductions and conclusions

Whichever approach you adopt, there are two features of a presentation that you need to prepare carefully and get right: the introduction and the conclusion.

Introductions

The introduction is your bait and if you cast it right, you can catch your audience right at the start. Remember: they could be meeting you for the first time and research shows that we form a strong first impression of a person very quickly. What's the best way to make sure they form a positive image of you? Here's what you need to do.

1 Before you start, chat to early arrivers. Introduce yourself and learn their names.

2 Welcome the audience with a smile and tell them you're about to begin.

3 Introduce yourself with your name and your job title.

4 Introduce your topic and give them an idea of the content.

5 Say how long the presentation will last and if you prefer questions during your presentation or at the end.

6 Tell them if you've got handouts or if the slides will be made available after the presentation.

If an audience feels that the presenter is in charge of the situation, they'll relax and enjoy themselves. And so will you.

Conclusions

How do you feel if a film ends weakly? However good the rest of it was, you're left with a feeling of disappointment. The same is true of presentations so work on your conclusion until it feels powerful. Here are three patterns you can follow.

1 Summarise the key points, conclude with a recommendation, distribute any handouts and thank the audience. This is best when the main purpose of the presentation is to give the audience neutral information.

2 Summarise the key points, conclude with a recommendation and invite questions from the audience. This works well if you want to sell something, such as a product or a service. The questions will give you an opportunity to drum home the benefits of what you're selling.

3 Summarise the key points, conclude with a dramatic statement and thank the audience. This is for when you're trying to persuade your audience that change is necessary. The dramatic statement emphasises the dangers of not following your recommendations, or shows them the promised land they will enter if they follow them: *If we ignore the dangers of global warming, central London will be under water by 2050.*

Normally, it's not a good idea to write out your presentation in full. But with your conclusion, it can help to build your confidence to write it and then practise reading it aloud to yourself until you feel sure about its impact. When it's time for the real thing, put your notes aside and give it all you've got!

Using visual aids

A presentation without any visual aids apart from the speaker's face is feasible but demanding for those of us who are not blessed with film-star good looks. We need visual aids to:

■ keep the audience interested and curious about our topic

■ focus attention on key points

■ make these points more memorable.

Whatever medium you use to present your material, these are the areas you need to pay attention to when creating your visual aids: text, font, colour, pictures, graphs and charts.

Text

A large part of your message is carried by text so pay careful attention to how you handle the words on your slides. Remember the acronym **KISS** (**K**eep **I**t **S**hort and **S**imple) at all times. Don't worry about full sentences; key words are all that are needed. Look at these examples.

■ **Bad:** *Sales increased by 15% in the first six months of this year.*
   Good: *Sales Jan–June: +15%*

■ **Bad:** *The rise in the number of employees will be in the region of 20% annually for the next five years.*
   Good: *Employee expansion: +20% p.a. –> 2019*

Using key words or numbers means you can avoid reading from your slide and yet still keep the thread of your argument.

Font

The only thing more depressing than a former Big Brother contestant opening a new local supermarket is a presentation where all the slides are covered by line after line of tiny text in a miniscule font size. A useful guideline to follow when preparing your slides is the 7 × 7 rule: no slide should have more than seven lines of text, and each line should have a maximum of seven words.

If you follow the 7 × 7 rule, you can keep your font size large, preferably 24 pt for text and 32 pt for headings. You may need to vary this if you include a chart or picture. To make sure your text is large enough to read comfortably, print out a copy of your slide and put it on the floor at your feet. If you can read it, your audience should be able to read it when it's on screen.

Use a simple clear sans serif font like Arial or Gill Sans MT, which are easy to read. Serif fonts such as Times New Roman or Book Antiqua have curly ends to the letter strokes. These are designed to guide the eye from one letter to the next, which makes them good for reading a book or article but not for slides. Finally, nobody will take you seriously if you use quirky fonts like Comic Sans MS in a presentation. Keep these for creating children's birthday party invitations.

Colours

When creating slides for the computer or flipcharts for the wall, you might be tempted to go overboard and use all the colours available for your text. The result can end up looking like a seven-year-old child's face after they've got hold of their mum's make-up. Not a pretty sight.

For text, avoid light colours such as yellow, orange and green as they are very difficult to read. Stick to black or dark blue on light backgrounds. However, with slides, it can be useful to switch to white on a dark background for headings. This ensures that they'll be noticed and will contrast nicely with the main body of the slide.

If you want to use colours, use them to frame text boxes or as the fill colour for symbols such as pie charts or arrows. They can be useful if you want to emphasise a point that is particularly important.

Pictures

If you see the words *London 2012*, what pictures come into your head? Jessica Ennis with a Union Jack? Usain Bolt in his victory pose? Pictures are powerful but you need to be careful in their selection. They should support your words and inform the audience, not distract them. It's also important to remember that simply downloading pictures from the internet can lead to copyright problems, while clipart can make for a bland and boring presentation. Here are some key points to remember.

■ Make sure the pictures you use are relevant to the point you want to make and the quality is good.

■ Don't try to illustrate every point. A couple of well-chosen pictures in an entire presentation can be more effective than hundreds. Also, if you're using software like PowerPoint, too many images will increase the size of the presentation. This can lead to problems if you want to email it to people. From a home computer a 5MB presentation can usually be emailed easily.

■ Don't use cartoon clipart of people. It generally looks amateurish.

■ Think about using your own photos: landscapes, modes of transport, buildings, plants – they can all be used to suggest concepts such as visions, goals or growth. Best of all, as they're your pictures, you don't have to worry about copyright issues.

Remember: finding something suitable can take time and you need to calculate this into your preparation. But when you get the right picture, the effect can be incredible.

Graphs and charts

Particularly when showing graphs or charts, it's helpful to put yourself in the shoes of your audience. You know what they're meant to show, but will they? Make sure the detail is not too small for people to see, and think carefully about how you can explain what the figures, bars or lines represent. Then, before your presentation, practise explaining them to somebody who is unfamiliar with the topic and answer any questions they have. To reduce the risk of confusion, follow these steps.

1 **Use the one-one rule:** Use only one graph or chart per slide to get just one idea across.

2 **Integrate the visual carefully:** Prepare the audience for what they're going to see so that they are alert and ready for what is coming up: *Let's have a look at a graph that will illustrate what I'm talking about.*

3 **Explain what they can see:** Once the graph is up on the screen or on the flipchart, leave a small pause so the audience can begin to analyse it. Don't rush them. Then focus their attention on what's important and make sure there are no misunderstandings.

4 **Control what they can see:** If you're showing a bar graph that illustrates the change in turnover over a number of years, consider showing the bars for each year one after the other. This means the audience will look only at what you want them to and you can get your message over more easily.

Presentation notes

We all know those cool presenters who can deliver a presentation without any notes. How do they do it? Probably the first few times they had notes to help them so it's perfectly acceptable for you to have some to guide you initially. What are some of the do's and don't's?

Do:

■ Use the note-taking function available with a software program like PowerPoint. This enables you to print your slides with notes underneath to remind you what you're talking about.

■ Alternatively, use cards with the key points of your presentation on them. Have one card per slide so that when you change your slide, you also change your card. Make sure you label your cards so you don't get confused.

■ Do a dry run of your presentation with a friend, once with notes and once without. Ask your friend whether you really need notes. Could you manage without them?

Don't:

■ Write out your complete presentation. This will stop you being spontaneous.

■ Bury your head in your notes so you don't have to look at the audience.

■ Read aloud everything on your slides. Firstly, your audience are able to read for themselves. Secondly, if you're reading from slides, you aren't looking at your audience.

Live demos

What does a fruit seller in a market do to convince you to buy her wares? She cuts up some of her products into small samples for you to try. All your senses are activated and you probably end up spending your money.

Of course, we rely heavily on sight to acquire information. But a presenter who not only shows his audience what he's talking about but also gives them something to handle can be very effective. Sometimes this is easy: if you're giving a presentation about a food product, pass around samples. But if you're presenting a new software product or a service, you have to be more creative. Occasionally, it can be helpful to think about what your product is *not*. For instance, suppose your software enables electronic billing. You can contrast its efficiency and environmental friendliness with conventional paper and post billing by having a big stack of old bills and envelopes on a table beside you and telling the audience that the paper pile represents just one little megabyte on your computer.

Of course, if you do a live demo of your product or service, you're doing the same as the fruit seller in the market – showing the audience why they should buy into what you're selling. But remember: with a live demo, you need to spend even more time checking your equipment in advance to eliminate any problems. Nothing will destroy your presentation confidence quite as successfully as a dead screen.

The naked presentation

Have you ever had the dream where you're back at college and your tutor asks you to stand up to answer a question and when you do, you realise you're naked? Well, giving an impromptu presentation without visual aids can be like that. And it's not uncommon; you could suddenly be asked in a meeting to explain your work to visitors or to senior management. Here's how to handle the situation.

1 Smile and look at the people, not the floor – or the table, if everyone's sitting round a table.

2 Keep your hands in front of you. Imagine you're holding a pen.

3 Tell 'em your name (slowly, so they can hear it – think 007: *My name's Bond. James Bond*).

4 Tell 'em your position and what you're responsible for.

5 Tell 'em what you're working on at the moment.

6 Tell 'em what's challenging about the task.

A good introduction might sound like this: *Hello. My name's Jenny. Jenny Kingsfield. I'm a team assistant and responsible for putting the project data into the weekly project report. At the moment I'm also organising an event for the project members so that they can get to know each other better. It's hard to find a date that everyone can agree on so I have to …*

Presenting online

Increasingly, it's necessary to do online presentations. An advantage is that costs are reduced. If people can watch a presentation online, there are no travel expenses. The disadvantage is that people often multi-task during online presentations so the message is not necessarily transferred efficiently. If you have to present online, bear the following in mind.

- Insist that you have a moderator who manages the technical aspects for you. If things go wrong, you won't be able to sort them out and give your presentation at the same time.

- Try to interact with your audience. Most platforms allow you to use multiple-choice questionnaires or to ask *yes/no* questions. Your audience click their answers back to you. This will keep them focused on the presentation.

- The platform normally has a chat function scrolling down the right side of the screen, next to your slides. Keep an eye on this because you can get a feeling for whether the audience is following you or not. If not, you can repeat or rephrase something.

Although online presentations are not ideal, there is something cool about talking to people in Argentina, Germany and Zambia, all at the same time. However, when setting up an online presentation, bear time zones in mind and ensure the time is convenient for all participants.

Sounding Pro

So what might you say during your presentation? Here are some options that will work in most situations.

Opening a presentation: explaining the topic	*Today I'd like to talk about … / My subject today is …*
Giving an overview of your presentation	*Firstly, I'd like to talk about … / Secondly, I want to tell you how … / Thirdly/Finally I'll show you …*
Giving ground rules to your audience	*Feel free to ask any questions. / Please save your questions for the end.*
Introducing flipcharts or slides	*On the next slide we can see … / If you look at the chart here, you can see …*
Explaining advantages and disadvantages	*The strength of X is … / The big advantage of X is … / The difficulty with X is … / The problem with X is …*
Summarising your points	*So, to sum up, … / So, to recap, …*
Concluding your presentation	*In conclusion, … / To conclude my presentation today, …*
Giving impromptu introductions	*Hello. My name's Jenny. Jenny Kingsfield. I'm a team assistant and responsible for …*

Key take-aways

Think about the things you will take away from Step 2 and how you will implement them.

Topic	Take-away	Implementation
How to decide what type of presentation approach to use	• *Think about audience expectations.* • *Consider the pros and cons of different approaches.*	• *Talk to colleagues about expectations.* • *Find a method that works for me.*
How to deliver powerful introductions and conclusions		
How to use the Classical approach		
How to use the FAB approach		
How to use the Persuasive approach		
How to use text in visual aids		
How to use colour in visual aids		
How to use pictures effectively		
How to introduce visuals effectively		
How to handle an impromptu presentation		
How to give a presentation online		

ASSESS THE VENUE AND EQUIPMENT

'If there are any of you at the back who do not hear me, please don't raise your hands because I'm also near sighted.'
— W.H. Auden, writer (1907–1973)

Five ways to succeed

- Plan early.
- Find out what resources are available to you.
- Create checklists.
- Visit the venue in advance.
- Make friends with resident technical staff.

Five ways to fail

- Rely on others for information about the venue.
- Miscalculate audience numbers.
- Don't prepare sufficient handouts.
- Don't check technical equipment.
- Don't arrange back-up support.

The venue

You won't have much influence on the choice of venue but you can make the best of what's available. The factors that you need to consider are room size, room shape, furniture, seating arrangements and lighting.

Room size

What would you rather have: twenty people in a small room or twenty people with enough space to spread out and be comfortable? For the audience, the second option sounds more attractive but that's not necessarily true for the speaker. If your room is crowded, it can be uncomfortably warm but the atmosphere is normally better. If people are spread out too much, your presentation can feel flat and you'll find it difficult to connect with the audience. As a rule of thumb, the closer you are to your audience, the better. We'll look at that point later on when we talk about seating arrangements.

Room shape

The owner of the building probably won't allow you to knock down or put up any walls for your presentation so you need to make sure you've thought in advance how best to fit the audience, yourself and any technical equipment into the space available. Look at it critically and discuss with others what's the best that can be done.

Furniture

There may be little you can do about the furniture but it's worth checking what's possible with the facility's management in advance. Before you speak to them, make sure you have a clear idea of what the participants will be doing. If they're just going to listen and take notes, then tables and chairs make sense. However, if you want to have a workshop and ask people to move around or talk to each other in groups, tables can be a nuisance. See if you can have them removed.

What do you need for yourself? If you're using a portable multimedia projector and computer, you'll need a table to place them a suitable distance away from the projection screen or wall. You might also like somewhere to put your prompt cards and a glass of water. Alternatively, if you're giving a presentation at a regular internal meeting, there's little you can do to change the furniture. These meetings are usually round a table so you'll be seated as you present.

Seating arrangements

The optimal seating arrangement can help to make your presentation a success. Here are some tips for possible layouts.

■ **Rows of desks and chairs:** This is practical because a lot of people fit into a small space, but it's reminiscent of school and there's a barrier between you and the audience. If you're faced with this layout, make sure that everybody sits as close to the front as possible. If you know how many people are coming, remove extra chairs before your presentation.

■ **Tables-and-chairs horseshoe:** This layout allows people to see your slides or flipcharts and take notes as you talk, but the tables are a barrier. Minimise that barrier by moving around in the centre of the horseshoe from time to time.

■ **Tables-and-chairs islands:** With this layout, two or three tables are pushed together and five to six people sit at each island. The islands are dotted around the room. This allows your audience to interact with each other and take notes. It also allows you to walk between the islands, which eliminates the barrier between you and the audience. However, it can be difficult for everybody to have a good sight of your slides or flipchart.

■ **Chairs horseshoe:** This is the best and most flexible arrangement. You can move around the centre and interact with the audience, and the audience can move their chairs and discuss points with each other. Everybody should be able to see the slides. If you know the number of people in the audience in advance, you can move the chairs and determine where people will sit. The disadvantage is if people want to take notes but we'll look at solutions later.

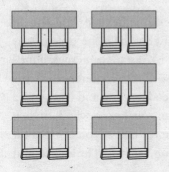

Rows of desks and chairs

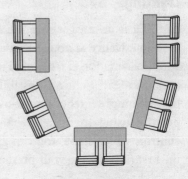

Tables–and–chairs horseshoe

Tables–and–chairs islands

Chairs horseshoe

Lighting

Lighting is an area where you have to be flexible. You should look in advance at your room at roughly the same time of day your presentation is scheduled to check out the windows, blinds and overhead lighting possibilities. Many conference rooms have dimmer switches for the overhead lighting and you should practise using them beforehand so you know which switch controls which light. You can guarantee that if you try this for the first time during your presentation, you won't be able to find the right one!

If you're giving a computer-based presentation with a projector onto a screen, have the part of the room where your screen is fairly dark. That way the eyes of the audience will be drawn – like moths – to the light from the screen. The part of the room where the audience is sitting should be well-lit; firstly so that they can see well enough to take notes if they want to, and secondly so that nobody gets sleepy.

If you're using a screen, at a trade fair for example, make sure it's positioned so that sunlight from the windows does not make it difficult to see.

In general, be aware of the effect that bad lighting can have on your presentation. If you notice during your presentation that the lighting has changed in some way and your audience suddenly has problems seeing your slides, pause and do something about it. They'll appreciate your interest in their well-being.

Equipment and technical support

The equipment necessary for your presentation will form a major part of your logistical preparations. Used well, it can help you to communicate your message powerfully but if you don't prepare carefully, it can ruin all your hard work. We'll look at two different areas: electronic equipment (computer, multimedia projector, screen, monitors, remote control, microphone, speakers, plugs, adaptors, extension leads, internet connections) and flipcharts/pinboards. You may not have any equipment in the case of regular internal meetings, where your colleagues may be reading paperwork they have received in advance of the meeting as you present.

Electronic equipment

Most presentations today are given using electronic equipment, and the first thing you need to consider is where you intend to store your presentation: on PowerPoint or some other format. Nowadays it's possible to prepare your presentation online and store it in Google, for example, so it's not actually on your own computer at all. This means that when you launch your presentation, you need to have internet access. This is risky: there are many possibilities for things to go wrong and it makes more sense to take a conservative approach and have the presentation on your hard disk or a USB stick.

■ **Computers:** The safest option is to use your own computer for the presentation. This isn't always possible because if you're one of a number of presenters, the organisers might want to have all the presentations on one computer from the start. This helps them because no time is wasted connecting and disconnecting separate computers. If this is the case, get the organisers to check that your presentation displays correctly with their hardware.

■ **Multimedia projectors:** In the past there were sometimes compatibility problems between different computers and projectors. This is becoming increasingly rare but it's important to check in advance that the projector works with your computer and presentation program. Check that the image projected is sharp enough. If not, you can usually focus the lens. Then have a look at the colours: they can sometimes appear differently on the screen from the way they look on your computer. If that is the case, you may need to adjust the colours in your presentation. Make sure you allow for that possibility when you prepare your preparation.

■ **Screens:** Ideally, you will have a wall-mounted screen. In that case, you just need to make sure that your projector angle is adjusted so that it shows your presentation at the correct height. If you have a portable screen, position it in the correct place before starting: portable screens can be difficult to move and you don't want to try doing it in front of an audience. It's guaranteed to choose that moment to topple over.

■ **Monitors:** As always, check in advance if the monitor is compatible with your computer. In general, monitors are very attractive because of the high picture quality, which means that your presentation appears exactly as on your computer. Some of the more sophisticated monitors also have swipe technology so that you can move backwards and forwards in your presentation by swiping. This technique is fun but should be practised so that you can do it confidently. There's nothing worse than frantically swiping the wrong part of the monitor while the slide obstinately refuses to move. If you find this to be the case, try cleaning the surface.

■ **Remote control:** A remote control allows you to click forwards and backwards through your slides without having to touch the computer. Remote controls normally have other functions built in that are worth exploring in advance. The laser pointer, for example, allows you to highlight something important on your slide. If you do use that function, make sure you leave the light on the item you wish to highlight for between five to ten seconds. For the audience, it's very irritating when all they can see is a little red or green spot bouncing seemingly at random around the screen. Some remotes also allow you to blank out the screen. This can be useful if you want the participants to talk to each other or listen to you and not look at the screen for a while.

- **Microphone and speakers:** There are disadvantages to using a microphone and speakers. They are yet more pieces of technical equipment that can go wrong, and feedback can cause the system to deafen you and your audience.

However, if the room and the audience are large and if your voice isn't that big, it's a good idea to use a sound system. If possible, select a headset or a clip-on microphone, which leaves your hands free and ensures your audience can hear you. If you have to work with a hand microphone, make sure you hold it close enough to your mouth so that your voice is picked up properly. There's nothing funnier than a speaker waving a hand microphone around like a giant lollipop while nobody can hear a word.

If you want to play audio or video, perhaps from the internet, you'll definitely need external speakers as in-built computer speakers will not be powerful enough.

■ **Plugs, extension leads, adaptors:** These seemingly small details can cause last-minute panics if you don't sort them out in advance. When you check your room, check where the plugs are positioned for your electrical equipment as this may affect how you organise the seating. You must think about how many plugs you need, for example if you want to run a computer, projector and speakers at the same time.

If the plugs are badly placed or your cables are too short, make sure you have a suitable extension cable. Just be careful that it doesn't stretch across a piece of floor that somebody can trip over. If it's possible for somebody to do so, they will.

Finally, be careful about adaptors. If you're running your presentation from an iPad or an Apple computer, you might need a special adaptor to connect with the projector. Make sure you have the right pieces in place and that they all work.

■ **Internet connections:** If you want to include something from the internet in your presentation, you need to make sure the internet connections you have are good. Ideally, use an internet cable connection. If that's not possible, check that the wireless connection is powerful enough in advance. It's advisable to have a plan B ready in case something goes wrong and whatever it is that you want to display won't do so. There's nothing more impressive than a presenter who can calmly carry on with an alternative approach when the technology collapses.

Flipcharts and workshop material

You may feel that what you're presenting will work better with a flipchart than with a computer. However, flipcharts need careful planning too.

- **Flipchart pens, pins and cards:** Make sure all of these materials are readily available and in good condition if you plan to use them. Are the pens full of ink, for example? As always, think in advance about what you need, how much you need and where you can get it from.

- **Flipchart paper:** Always have more flipchart paper than you think you'll need. Running out of paper before you've finished is unprofessional and could ruin your presentation.

- **Flipchart stands:** If you have a flipchart stand on wheels, it's easy to move around. More often they have a tripod arrangement that can be raised or lowered. Be careful: it is heavy and difficult to move so get somebody to help you to get it in position before your presentation. You don't want it collapsing on top of your audience.

- **Pinboards:** These are large cork-based boards on which you can pin cards with key words. They're also great for group work; you can give each group a pinboard and a pile of cards that they can then use to brainstorm answers to a question or problem. Pinboards are light and easy to move around so a group can work on something and then bring their board to the front of the room to explain it to everybody.

Technical support

The moment you agree to give a presentation you should be trying to make a new BFF (Best Friend Forever) – the person responsible for technical support and equipment at the venue. A technical BFF can contribute enormously to your success so it's worthwhile cultivating a good relationship with them. Explain what you want and listen respectfully to their suggestions but if they don't like what you say, be persistent. For example, if you want to use an iPad for your presentation and they claim it won't work with their projector, stick to your guns as long as possible without making yourself too unpopular and try to find a technical solution.

Often it's a question of planning something sufficiently far in advance with your BFF. Ordering equipment, making sure internet connections work – these things take time to arrange. In particular, try to arrange with your BFF a dry run of your presentation in the room scheduled for the presentation, using the same equipment planned for the real thing. This is not always possible but if you can make it happen, it's worth it. A dry run will pinpoint any technical bugs that need to be fixed and will boost your confidence enormously. Make sure you have a mobile number so you can get hold of your BFF if something goes wrong at the last minute.

And finally, when it's all over, make sure you thank your BFF. That way your next presentation will be much easier.

Materials for the audience

However good your presentation, your audience will appreciate material that they can refer to later to remind them of what you said. There are five different forms this supplementary material can take, each requiring a different level of input from you as a presenter.

Electronic version

This is the simplest approach and involves making your presentation available in electronic form after the event. If you've prepared your presentation in PowerPoint, it's advisable to change your document into PDF format before sending it by email to participants or uploading it to your company's intranet. You should do this for two reasons. Firstly, a PDF document is smaller than a PowerPoint document and is therefore easier to send. Secondly, as a PDF, it is not possible for somebody to simply take your presentation and claim it as their own. An advantage of this approach is its ease; you simply forward what you've already prepared and what the audience has already seen. The disadvantage is that you can't guarantee that they will open and print out your presentation.

Handouts

If you don't have too large an audience, one option is to prepare hard copies of your presentation. You simply have to know how many people are likely to attend (always print a couple of extra copies – just in case!) and make sure your audience knows that you will be distributing print copies of the complete presentation. However, be careful: distributing your handouts at the beginning of your presentation can be distracting; people may pay more attention to your handout and less attention to what you are saying.

An attractive feature of PowerPoint is the possibility to create condensed pages of your presentation by selecting *Handout notes* in the print program. If you select the option of three slides per page, the presentation is printed out with three slides per page plus four lines next to each slide, where the participant can write their own comments. This is particularly useful if your presentation venue has no tables so your participants can't make lots of notes. It is also helpful because they can personalise what they take away from the presentation. As a result, they can identify with it more strongly. But note: this approach doesn't add to your presentation. If you followed the KISS formula (Keep It Short and Simple) described in Step 2, some of the slides might seem cryptic two weeks later. If you think that might be the case, the next three options may be more appropriate.

Flyers

A flyer is not simply a repetition of your presentation; it is more like an executive summary of the content. It should list each of your key points with a supporting fact and finish with a statement expressing your conclusion and any action you think people should take. Most word processing programs have a template that you can use to create a flyer. You simply select what you feel to be the key messages from your presentation and complete the boxes. This can be printed out and given to the audience.

The advantage of a flyer is that you can distribute it in advance and it will not distract the audience from your presentation. It's more likely to support the message you want to put across. It's less cumbersome than a complete printout of the presentation and therefore more attractive to the participants. The disadvantage is that you can include only a limited amount of supporting information.

Full documentation

As we already saw in Step 2, the slides you produce for your presentation are a vastly reduced form of what you actually say. The reason for this is purely pragmatic: audiences will not be able to read your slides if you have too much text on them. The result is that quite often the slides are not actually of much use to anybody after the presentation as the bullet points alone do not provide much of a clue to the real content. If you're providing training or explaining a process that the audience needs to understand in detail, you'll need to provide a full explanation of the topic. The slides you generated for the presentation can provide a good basis for this documentation. All you need to do is flesh out the bullet points with more detail. This approach creates a clear, professional distinction between the presentation slides and the documentation.

Flipchart photo report

If you do a flipchart-based presentation, you should also make a photo report available to the audience. This is a complete set of the flipcharts or of the pinboards that the session generates. Use a digital camera to photograph them, transfer the pictures onto your computer and then email them to the participants. Because of all the images, your photo report will be quite large. Therefore, it's a good idea to compress the file using compression software like WinZip. This will make it easier and quicker to download.

Presentation timing

Is your presentation one of a series of talks? Will yours be followed by another presentation? If you are one of a number of presenters, you need to consider audience presentation tolerance. For example, it's difficult talking to people shortly before lunch because their attention is probably focused more on food than on what you have to say. Of course, it's also tricky *after* lunch when everybody wants to have a siesta.

When you know the schedule, think about the potential consequences of that time slot. It'll help you to structure your presentation and make sure the effect of your message is not diminished. For example, if you have the post-lunchtime presentation slot, include activities where people have to interact with their neighbour. This will discourage sleepiness and keep your audience on their toes. Another tricky time slot is the last one before the end of the day. Sometimes people have to leave early for another meeting or go home. Be tolerant of this and don't allow yourself to be put off. Try to make sure you finish delivering your content ten minutes before the scheduled end and fill the last part answering questions from those people who don't want to leave.

Sounding Pro: A pre-presentation checklist

Whenever you have to give a presentation, use this checklist to make sure you have considered the logistical aspects of your presentation in advance.

Task	Performed	When	Comment
Talk to technical support staff/facility management.			
Check room.			
Check lighting possibilities.			
Check possible seating arrangements.			
Check technical equipment.			
Do a dry run with the presentation equipment.			
Check/Order additional materials, e.g. flipchart material.			
Arrange handout material for audience.			
Arrange catering.			

Key take-aways

Think about the things you will take away from Step 3 and how you will implement them.

Topic	Take-away	Implementation
Exploiting a venue's physical characteristics to aid my presentation	• Check practical details at venue, e.g. lights, plugs and shape of room.	• Make sure I ask in advance where I am giving my presentation.
Deciding which seating arrangement is most appropriate for my presentation		
How to exploit the lighting possibilities of the venue		
Making sure technical aspects have been checked and are in place		
How to prepare for a flipchart presentation		
Making sure technical support is in place for my presentation		
How to plan and organise handout material for the audience		

Step 4

MAKE AN IMPACT

'Three things matter in a speech: who says it, how it is said and what is said. And of the three, the last matters least.'
— John Morley, first Viscount of Blackburn (1855–1934)

Five ways to succeed

- Find examples of good speakers on the internet.
- Learn the language of presentations.
- Practise a variety of rhetorical devices.
- Try out different techniques for delivering a message.
- Get feedback on your performance.

Five ways to fail

- Rely on spontaneity to carry you through.
- Talk too quietly.
- Talk in a monotone.
- Talk too fast.
- Prepare only the content and not the delivery.

Signpost language

In Step 2 we looked at the language you need to introduce yourself and your topic, to refer to any visual aids and to deliver a powerful conclusion. But in the main body of the presentation, you also need to make it plain to your audience what you are doing as you move from point to point. You can do this by using signpost language. Here are some examples.

- **So, first of all,** *let's take a look at the current software in use by the accounting team, Cost Controller. This is …*

- **Moving on to my next point,** *we can see that the hotline support offered by Cost Controller will stop at the end of the year. This means that …*

- **I'd now like to turn to** *the question of security. This is an issue that is increasingly relevant because …*

- **Which brings me to my next point:** *costs. By investing now we can …*

- **So finally, I'd like to outline** *the next steps we need to take …*

These signpost phrases indicate to the audience that a new point is coming up. People's attention span is short – roughly fifteen minutes per subject. Signpost phrases say: *Hey, wake up and listen to this. It's something new!*

Rapport language

We already saw in Step 2 that using *we* instead of *you* helps an audience to feel included. You can help your audience to identify even more positively with what you're saying by using two simple techniques.

Question tags

With careful preparation we've seen that giving presentations can be fun, *haven't we?* Question tags like these are useful for gently pushing our audience along the path we want them to take. They imply that everybody agrees with what is being said and you (the presenter) are just confirming this obvious fact. The listener has to make a conscious effort to reject what you're saying, which is harder than just going along with it. Here are some more examples.

- *It's obvious, **isn't it?***

- *We need to remember the risks, **don't we?***

- *We can't delay, **can we?***

- *We've included everything, **haven't we?***

- *We'll need to change our processes, **won't we?***

- *It doesn't work, **does it?***

Try not to use more than one question tag per point in your presentation. If it's obvious what you're doing, the audience will rebel and refuse to listen. And we don't want that, do we?

Negative questions

Wouldn't you welcome a technique that allowed you to reach out to your audience? Of course you would! When you use a negative question like the one above, you make a direct appeal to the audience for their support. You can use this approach not only in presentations but any time you want to convince somebody of something. For example:

- ■ *Shouldn't we* be planning this together?

- ■ *Isn't it* time to stop now?

- ■ *Can't we* resolve this issue together?

- ■ *Haven't the results* shown that the system works?

As with question tags, you should avoid using negative questions too often as they can begin to annoy the audience. But they can be very effective if slipped in once or twice in a presentation.

Intensifying language

To make an idea more powerful, we can give it 'oomph' by adding intensifiers. To illustrate the point, read this paragraph aloud:

The new software version is better than its predecessor because it is faster and can handle large amounts of data. The support costs will drop because it is stable and so less time than before will be lost due to technical problems. Data security is improved because of the use of encryption. This means it's unacceptable not to use this new version. And it's not expensive either.

Now read this version with intensifiers and hear the difference:

*The new software version is **far** better than its predecessor because it is **so much** faster and can handle **extremely** large amounts of data. The support costs will drop **dramatically** because it is **extremely** stable and so **significantly** less time than before will be lost due to technical problems. Data security is **vastly** improved because of the use of encryption. This means it's **just** unacceptable not to use this new version. And it isn't **even** expensive either.*

There are many intensifiers but it's a good idea to avoid using ones that are associated with teen-speak, such as *totally* or *awesome*. The number of intensifiers you use depends on your style. Do you prefer an understated approach or are you more extravagant? Go with what feels natural.

Wowing the audience

So far we've looked at the language you need for a solid presentation. Now we're going to look at how you can turn a good presentation into a brilliant one by using various rhetorical devices. The first thing you need to do is get your audience hooked.

When a presenter starts speaking, the audience is at its most expectant. They're hoping to enjoy themselves but they may be afraid they won't. You can win them over almost instantly by using one of these three techniques.

1 The amazing fact

Did you know that every thirty seconds somebody in the world buys a bottle of Chanel Number 5? No? Well, you'll probably never forget it now. Amazing-but-true facts are a great way to get your audience to pay attention; however, you do need to show a plausible connection to your topic. The Chanel fact can be used to demonstrate the power of a brand name, for example. Search the internet for unusual facts and figures or have a look in *Guinness World Records* and see what you can use for your presentation.

2 The challenge

If a rogue virus infected all your company's computers tomorrow, how would you deliver goods to your customers? This kind of challenge question is a great way to start a presentation. Like the beginning of a good thriller, you confront your audience with a horror scenario and the rest of the presentation shows them how to get out of trouble. In the example given here, the presenter could go on to explain the seriousness of the situation, point out the disastrous consequences for the company and then explain the steps that have to be taken before unveiling the solution. Make sure the disaster you depict is plausible and by the end of your presentation you'll have the audience cheering. Just a word of caution: first make sure none of your audience has a weak heart condition!

3 The anecdote

All good presenters are essentially storytellers because stories get an audience involved and intrigued in the topic. Good presenters also know that relating a personal anecdote will make what they say far more plausible to an audience than simply using data. Data can win over the mind but a story can win over the heart.

One way to find relevant stories when you're preparing a presentation is to think about your own experience of the topic. Have you tried the product yourself? Were you helped by the service you're describing? What was your first day in the company like? What is something you'll never forget about the people you work with? Your audience will be far more responsive if they can see that your presentation has a personal element to it and it'll help them to identify with what you're saying. Here are some do's and don't's for storytelling.

Do:

- Keep it short.

- Make sure it's relevant. Your audience will notice if you're wasting their time.

- Make sure it has a beginning, middle and end.

- Practise telling it. Stories are like jokes – they need rehearsing.

Don't:

- Tell a story that is in any way offensive to the audience. And do remember: with YouTube, Facebook and Twitter your audience are not the only people in the room with you.

- Use more than two stories in a presentation.

- Allow the stories to push the key messages of your presentation into the background.

The power of three

In Step 1 we looked at the importance of clustering your points under a maximum of three headings so that people can remember the content of the presentation better. Our brains are full of phrases to do with the number three. Here are a few.

- *Three's a crowd.*
- *Three wishes.*
- *Two out of three ain't bad.*
- *Three strikes and you're out.*
- *Third time lucky.*

The power of three can be applied to other aspects of a presentation. Some great speakers created their most powerful messages using three-part sentences and phrases.

- *'There are three types of lies: lies, damned lies and statistics.'* — Benjamin Disraeli, British politician (1804–81)
- *'Justice, goodwill and brotherhood.'* — Martin Luther King Jr
- *'Government of the people, by the people, for the people.'* — Abraham Lincoln, American politician (1809–1865)

The first part of a three-part sentence captures the listener's attention, the second builds the tension and the third provides the release or explanation. Beginning, middle and end. But how can you exploit this phenomenon? You need to triple your adjectives, build patterns into your sentence structure and practise, practise, practise.

Adjective tripling

We looked earlier at the use of intensifiers; tripling your adjectives works as a super-intensifier. Read three versions of the sentence below aloud and hear how much more powerful the third one is.

■ *The new software is powerful.*

■ *The new software is fast and powerful.*

■ *The new software is effective, fast and powerful.*

Make sure that the key point you want to get across is the last one, in this case *powerful*. The three adjectives rolled into one sentence will make sure it sticks in your audience's mind.

Structure

When you want to answer a question – either one from your audience or one that you built into your presentation – a three-part answer can help, particularly if you keep to the same grammatical structure or pattern for each part. Compare these two answers.

■ *We can increase our efficiency if we use new software. Another possibility is to employ more staff. And then, of course, we could move to a cheaper office.*

■ *We can increase our efficiency **by using** new software, **by employing** more staff and **by moving** to a cheaper office.*

This use of the same grammatical structure or pattern makes it easier for your audience to process your message and gives it a greater chance of being accepted.

Practice

These techniques aren't difficult but you need to practise them until they sound uncontrived. Be patient: try them out and you'll be amazed at the results.

Using your voice

We've seen how to make your presentation more powerful by using an appropriate presentation structure and language and rhetorical tools, but what can you do with your voice?

To answer this question, think about another question. Have you ever listened to an interview with a singer you really admire and been disappointed at how flat and uninteresting they sound? The problem for some singers is that although they've been trained to *sing* words with meaning and feeling, they have difficulties doing the same when they're talking. The truth is that your presentation can have a superb structure, amazing content and utilise every rhetorical trick in the book, but if your delivery is monotonous and dull, nobody will listen to you. For some people, this is the biggest challenge of a presentation because they have to consciously control their delivery in a way that is not dissimilar to what an actor does. What makes giving a presentation different from acting is that you're working with your own words, not somebody else's. It isn't a question of trying to sound artificial, it's about maximising the impact of your presentation by using stress, pauses, intonation, emphasis, pace and volume effectively.

Stress

In English we normally stress the word at the end of a sentence, but what happens to the meaning of the sentence when we stress other words? Here are some examples.

■ *We'll finish analysing the data you asked for by* **tomorrow.** = You'll get the information you need tomorrow.

■ **We'll** *finish analysing the data you asked for by tomorrow.* = We'll be ready – but other people handling the same/other data won't be.

■ *We'll finish* **analysing** *the data you asked for by tomorrow.* = The analysis will be finished tomorrow but then the next step begins, for example, interpretation.

■ *We* **will** *finish analysing the data you asked for by tomorrow.* = Stop worrying! You'll get the information you need at the time agreed.

■ *We'll finish analysing the data* **you** *asked for by tomorrow.* = Your data will be ready – but not the data requested by somebody else.

■ *We'll finish analysing the data you* **asked** *for by tomorrow.* = We'll finish only the data that you specifically requested.

■ *We'll finish analysing the* **data** *you asked for by tomorrow.* = The data will be ready, but nothing else.

Stressing individual words is the easiest way to highlight the most important information in a sentence. You probably use this technique already without being aware of it. But now you are aware, look for opportunities to play with the meaning of a sentence when talking with friends. Stress will then become an effective technique you can use whenever you're giving a presentation.

Pauses

In front of an audience it's easy to panic and think that what you have to say isn't very interesting. Of course, you must make sure that your topic is relevant before you start preparing your presentation but in any case, you can be reassured by the fact that any topic can be made to sound more interesting through the intelligent use of pauses. The key to using pauses is to understand how our brain stores language. Look at these phrases and see if you can guess what the missing words are.

■ *Fish and ...*

■ *Hi, how are ...?*

■ *Thanks a ...!*

■ *What can I ... for you?*

■ *I'm afraid Mr Snow is in a ... Can I take a ...?*

Although grammatically it is possible to say *Fish and artichokes*, most of us will have finished that phrase with *chips*. This is because our brain doesn't build sentences out of individual words; it uses complete phrases or language chunks, some of which, like the last one, can be up to about eleven words long. They are stored that way in our brain so that they can be quickly and easily strung together without thinking. Imagine a typical conversation on Monday morning when people arrive at work. Most of it is made up of greeting chunks like this:

– *Morning.*

– *Morning*

– *Good weekend?*

– *Yeah, alright. You?*

For presentations we use language chunks to keep the audience on board as we talk to them.

77

Now look at these two parts of a presentation that have been 'chunked'. Read them aloud, stressing the words in bold and pausing for one second after each double slash //.

Introduction:

*Good **morning**, ladies and gentlemen.// Today I'd like to talk about// our new software development program.// First, I'll look at the **functions** of the software.// Then I'll examine the **costs**.// Finally, I'll say something about the data **security** features of this approach.*

Summary:

***So,**//to sum up my presentation **today,**//we looked at three important **factors**.//*

***One**://Would this software do the **job**?// The answer was clearly//**yes**.// **Two**://Would it cut **costs**? **Again,**//the answer was//**yes**. // **Three**://Would it increase our data security?//**Once** more,//the answer was//**yes**.*

These were not the only choices for stress and pauses that we could make. It would also be perfectly acceptable to add pauses after *First, Then* and *Finally* in the introduction. One simple way to practise working with chunks and pauses is to find a short newspaper article and try reading it aloud in different ways. For example, you could read it as:

- a bedtime story for a small child
- a radio news broadcast
- a horror story
- a comic story.

Doing this will help you to appreciate how much you can do to make your presentation interesting and motivating.

Intonation

An interesting feature of English compared to other European languages is that it uses a greater tone range, which means that in normal conversation the voice goes up and down a lot. It's difficult for non-native speakers to give a presentation in English because languages such as German, Italian and Spanish have different intonation patterns to ours so if you attend an English presentation by a non-native speaker, try and be supportive.

Our intonation shows how we feel about a particular subject. Try this small (very unscientific) experiment. Think of:

    a) a food you really hate

    b) somebody you think is really good-looking

    c) a piece of music you really love

    d) a film that sent you to sleep

    e) a person you dislike

Now imagine telling your best friend about them using only these sentences.

    a) food: *It's just disgusting!*

    b) person: *He/She's hot!*

    c) music: *This song is amazing!*

    d) film: *It was really boring.*

    e) person: *He/She's a real pain!*

Can you make them understand how emotional you feel about them? Do your feelings come across in your voice? Don't worry about sounding a bit theatrical. To a certain extent, you are on stage when you give a presentation and so you can legitimately ham it up a bit. The important thing to remember is that if you don't vary your intonation, you'll sound monotonous and boring and run the risk of your audience dozing off.

Now practise different intonation styles on these sentences. First, read them as if they were very boring; then as if they were the most important statements you'll ever make; and finally as if you were including them in a presentation to your boss. This exercise will give you a real feeling for what you are capable of doing with intonation.

- *What doesn't kill you makes you stronger.*

- *Bite off more than you can chew, then chew it. Plan more than you can do, then do it.*

- *Efficiency is intelligent laziness.*

- *The best defence against the atom bomb is not to be there when it goes off.*

- *A good scare is worth more to a man than good advice.*

- *The bigger they are, the harder they fall.*

- *He who fails to plan, plans to fail.*

Finally, a word of warning: language is not static; it is constantly changing. New words and phrases come into fashion and this also applies to intonation patterns. One of the most irritating developments in the UK over recent years has been that of the question intonation at the end of ordinary statements. The probable reason for this is a desire to get feedback from the listener but the result is that everything the speaker says sounds like a question. In a presentation it's very tiring to listen to and may alienate your audience. So make sure you aren't guilty of doing this yourself.

Emphasis

We've already seen how changing the stress in a sentence can have an impact on its meaning. In the examples on page 76, we focused on the main words that carry meaning in the sentences. We can do something similar with auxiliary verbs such as *is*, *are*, *will*, *was*, *were*, *has*, *have*, *had*, as well as negatives and the definite article (*the*). By emphasising these words, we can turn a neutral sentence into something more powerful, and this is especially useful if we wish to contradict somebody or disprove an assumption. For example:

Suggestion/Assumption	Emphatic response
The data won't be ready in time.	*We **will** finish analysing the data you asked for by tomorrow.*
We're uncompetitive.	*We **are** a strong competitor.*
Nobody expected this.	*It was **not** a surprise.*
He hasn't bought it.	*He **has** bought the company.*
It's a possible solution.	*It's **the** solution.*

Pace

We've already seen how pauses can be helpful in making sure your audience appreciates important points in your presentation. They can also be useful when contrasted with speech delivered at a fast pace. For example, if you pile on a series of facts one after the other to prove a particular point and then finish with a concluding statement delivered much more slowly, the impact is very effective. Look at this example.

Using-this-software-will-give-us-speed, data-security, greater-efficiency, the-ability-to-handle-vast amounts-of-data and greater-accuracy. // In **short**, *// it will make* **our** *company // **more** competitive // than* **any** *of our competitors.*

Volume

In Step 3 we looked at using microphones and speakers if you have a large audience and/or venue. If the equipment isn't available, you need to try to make sure that what you say can be heard at the back of the room. Do a dry run with a friend in advance to see if they can hear you; but as a general rule, try to imagine you're talking to a friend who has got headphones on and you want them to hear you.

Very occasionally, if you want to force people to listen carefully to a particular point, you can speak more softly. This normally forces people to pay more attention. However, only do this very briefly; if you overdo it, your audience will soon either start complaining or thinking about something else.

Sounding Pro

So what might you say during your presentation? Here are some options that will work in most situations.

Signposting	*So, first of all, let's look at the time schedule.* *Let's begin by examining the time schedule.*
	Moving onto my next point, costs will fall … *Turning now to the question of costs.* *As I mentioned earlier, we have to remember the costs.*
	So, finally I'd like to describe the solution. *To finish off today, I want to provide some answers.*
Creating rapport: question tags	*We're moving forward, aren't we?* *It isn't good enough, is it?*
Creating rapport: negative questions	*Don't we need a solution?* *Isn't it what we always wanted?*
Intensifying	*This is **actually** the best solution.* *It's **completely** unacceptable.* *The equipment wasn't **even** ready in time.*
Tripling adjectives	*He's mad, bad and dangerous to know!* *The software is fast, safe and easy to use.*
Structure	*To start this project, we need to find a project manager, to pick a team and to organise a kick-off meeting.*

Key take-aways

Think about the things you will take away from Step 4 and how you will implement them.

Topic	Take-away	Implementation
How to use signpost language	• *This makes clear to the audience that one point is finished and a new one has begun.*	• *Incorporate it into my planning.*
How to build audience rapport		
How to strengthen an idea		
How to hook an audience at the start of a presentation		
How to use tripling to maximise impact		
How to use voice stress to change meaning		
How to use pauses correctly		
How to integrate voice intonation, emphasis, pace and volume into my presentations		

Step 5

USE THE RIGHT BODY LANGUAGE

'The body says what words cannot.'
— Martha Graham, US dance choreographer
(1894–1991)

Five ways to succeed

- Start observing your body language in different situations.

- Ask colleagues for feedback on your body language.

- Video yourself and think what you could improve.

- Analyse the body language of other presenters.

- Always show your audience you respect them.

Five ways to fail

- Underrate the importance of body language.

- Think that technology is more important than you.

- Hide behind lecterns or tables.

- Avoid eye contact with your audience.

- Don't analyse your audience's body language.

The importance of body language

So far we've concentrated on the language, organisation and logistics of presentations. However, the difference between a successful and an unsuccessful presentation is what the audience sees in front of them.

Albert Mahrabian, Professor of Psychology at UCLA, carried out research in 1971 that came to some interesting conclusions. A presentation's success or failure depends roughly 7% on the content, 38% on the presenter's voice and about 55% on the presenter's body language. Body language has nothing to do with a presenter's physical attractiveness but with how convincingly they are able to use their physical presence to communicate their message. This can make an enormous difference. In 1960 John F. Kennedy and Richard Nixon took part in a televised debate in the run-up to the US presidential election. On his way to the studio, Nixon injured his knee. He refused make-up and stood behind his lectern in considerable pain, his face shiny with sweat under the studio lights. After the debate, radio listeners felt his arguments had been more convincing than Kennedy's. But what the larger TV audience saw was a man standing at an odd angle, sweating and looking as if his mind was elsewhere. The next day Kennedy's campaign took off and he won the election.

Breaking it down

A suggestion that is often made to a nervous presenter is to 'be natural'. This well-meant advice isn't terribly helpful because for most people being in front of an audience feels entirely unnatural. Suddenly, it's difficult to move, their face gets an expression of terror, their hands seem to become ten times larger and they've no idea where to put them any more.

In order to develop strategies for projecting good body language, it makes sense to break the body down into its key parts and examine them in turn. We can then put them back together again and work out some general guidelines for good body language.

The face

Your face is the most important visual aid that you've got as a presenter and it's important to realise that your audience will be subconsciously judging the plausibility of what you're saying based on what they see there. If you're talking about the great opportunities for school leavers in your company but all they can see on your face is a look of extreme boredom, they're not going to be lining up at the end to sign on the dotted line. It's crucial to remember that whenever there's a mismatch between the verbal and non-verbal information on display, the non-verbal is the one that is believed. So let's look carefully at your mouth and eyes.

Mouth: What do you do when you're pleased to see people? You smile, and even when you have a serious topic to address, you should always greet your audience with a smile. Of course, there's a big difference between a fake smile, which only moves the lips, and a genuine smile, which includes the eyes as well. But when you're giving a presentation, you should be happy that people want to listen to you so show your appreciation of their presence by giving them a smile as often as you feel is appropriate. Generally speaking, however, don't laugh. If you say something funny, carry on talking and allow the audience's laughter to interrupt you. Laughing at your own jokes is the best way to kill them dead.

Eye contact: How do you feel if you're talking to somebody who's wearing dark glasses with reflecting lenses? Most of us feel very uncomfortable and the reason is that we're uncertain whether we can believe what the person is saying because we can't see their eyes. This illustrates the important part that eyes play in communication and what an effective tool eye contact can be for a presenter. So how can we use our eyes? Here are some do's and don't's.

Do:

■ Look at your audience as much as possible. A presenter who avoids eye contact and only looks at their slides or notes may be seen as untrustworthy.

■ Bounce your gaze around the room. If you're unsure how to do this, try the following. Start by looking for everybody in glasses, then all the people you know, then everybody who is wearing something green, and so on.

■ Make sure you focus more on people you think might be sceptical about your topic. Your supporters don't need to be won over so you can safely spend less time on them. It's the others who need to be convinced so treat them to a full blast of eye power.

■ Focus on the triangle of eyes-and-nose on people's faces. This shows you find them interesting and you want to connect with them. If you notice that somebody isn't paying attention, let your eyes linger on them. They'll quickly notice and refocus on what you're saying.

Don't:

- Scan the room without settling on anybody, look out of the window or roll your eyes at a question. This makes people feel you're bored.

- Focus on people's foreheads rather than their eyes. This is always interpreted as a sign that you wish to dominate rather than engage with somebody and they will resent it.

- Focus on the triangle eyes-to-mouth. For many people, this is interpreted as displaying too much personal interest and could make them feel uncomfortable.

- Forget to combine eye contact with an occasional smile. This can be very powerful because it signals to the audience that you have supporters in the room. We're a sociable species who like to feel that we belong to the in-crowd. The eye contact-smile combination to a *number* of individuals scattered around the room makes everybody else feel that there's a gang that they ought to be in.

- Ignore the possibilities accorded by eye make-up if you're a woman. Making your eyes look larger can undoubtedly give you an advantage, as any stage actor will tell you.

Finally, though, a word of warning. Eye contact is very much culturally determined. There are many cultures where looking people in the eye is seen as showing a lack of respect. So always be aware of your audience and adjust your behaviour if you notice any negative reactions to the amount of eye contact you are making with them.

Arms and hands

Do you make gestures with your hands when you're on the phone? Isn't it a bit redundant? What this shows is that hand gestures are important in getting our message across. Even people who were born blind feel the need to make hand and arm gestures to communicate. However, there are big differences across different cultures in the way people use hand gestures (compare the Italians with the Japanese, for example) as well as between individuals. It's foolish to attempt to go radically against what's comfortable for you because you'll end up feeling false and your audience will notice. So consider these suggestions and see if you can use any of them to help you to maximise your performance.

■ If possible, use your hands and arms to point to key points on your slides. Generally speaking, this is better than using a laser pointer as it adds movement to the presentation, but it depends how far away you are from the screen. Use your whole arm and point from the shoulder, not the elbow – unless you want to look like a chicken.

■ When you want to list several points, hold up a hand and count them off clearly on your fingers.

■ Try not to wave your index finger around in the air to emphasise a point; it makes you look too teacherly. A good alternative is to press index finger and thumb together. This achieves the same effect without alienating your audience.

■ When you have nothing better to do with your hands, just leave them by your side. If that feels too weird, you can hold your remote control in your hands in front of you. And if you aren't using a remote control, a pen is a good substitute. Don't put your hands in your pockets. That doesn't look relaxed; it just looks sloppy.

■ Avoid standing with your arms crossed across your chest or your hands in front of your crotch. Both of these make you look defensive.

■ There will be times when you want everybody in your audience to feel included in what you're saying; open your arms with your palms up and imagine that you want to give them all a big hug.

■ If several people raise their hands to ask a question, it's best to use your whole hand to indicate who should ask first rather than pointing at them with your index finger. Best of all, to use their name if possible.

With practice, you'll work out which techniques work for you. These guidelines are not written in stone and you should adapt them to your particular situation. The main point to remember is that moving your hands and arms is helpful for your audience. They will be more likely to remember what you're saying if they can associate the verbal communication with a visual gesture so, without flailing your arms like a windmill, try to build movement into your presentation.

Legs

The next time you see an advertisement for a watch in a magazine, check what time it shows. Nine times out of ten it'll show the hands set at ten past ten. This is not a coincidence. In that position the hands appear to give the face of the watch a smile, which – as we've already discussed – induces a positive response from the viewer. You can use this example to help remind you how to stand when you're in front of an audience: face them full on and position your feet at ten past ten. This will automatically cause you to open your body out so that you exude an atmosphere of confidence that will inspire belief in what you have to say. Even if you're standing behind a lectern or desk, this effect will be instant. But why hide behind furniture? Of course, you shouldn't spend the whole time rushing from one side of the room to another like a marathon runner. But when possible, use your legs to get you out from behind tables and lecterns and up close to your audience because this is a great way to introduce more variety to what you're saying. When you're checking the venue before your presentation, check out first of all where your start point should be. Then see how much space you have to move around in – and *use* it.

Here are some possibilities.

- Move to the front of the area available to you for your presentation rather than staying at the back.

- If your audience is sitting in a semicircle, move down to about the halfway mark from time to time to deliver an important point. Then move back again.

- Move to the screen in order to point out a particularly significant point or figure, if possible with your finger.

- Move to one side of your screen to deliver positive information and to the other side for negative information.

- When somebody asks a question, move to stand in front of them (but not too close or you will intimidate them). This shows you really want to understand what they have to say.

It's possible that you may have to present sitting down. You can still use your face, eyes, arms and hands to maximise your performance even if you can't walk around.

Bringing it together

So far we've looked at individual parts of the body but there are also overall features of body language that can have a positive or negative impact on your performance. So which habits should you cultivate and which should you avoid?

Habits to cultivate

Posture: Always stand straight with your shoulders and head back, facing the audience with your feet apart and firmly planted on the ground. Do the same if you are sitting down. This will help you to radiate confidence and belief in your message.

Presentable appearance: We've talked about this before but its importance cannot be overestimated. It's not a case of being fashionably or expensively dressed; just be sure everything you wear is clean and well-ironed, shoes polished and hair tidy. Show your audience that you're a serious professional.

Enthusiasm: Show enthusiasm for your topic. Let the audience see from your body language – your smiles, the way you nod your head, how you use your arms to include them in everything – that you really believe in what you're saying because this will compensate for any number of slips in the smoothness of your delivery. Authentic enthusiasm is infectious so make sure you spread it.

Habits to avoid

Position: Always make sure that you're standing to one side of and level with the screen or flipchart so that you don't block the audience's view. This sounds like a no-brainer but it's amazingly easy to find yourself in a position that prevents half of the people present from seeing something important in your visual aids. Make sure you're aware of your audience's reaction to your slides and flips and if you suddenly see people craning their neck, move out of the way.

Fidgeting: A fidgety presenter is very irritating for the audience. There are people who keep clicking the ballpoint pen in their hand on and off and some men start playing with the coins or keys in their pockets. Such things can be very distracting so do your best to keep your hands still. To reduce the temptation to fidget, remove everything from your pockets before you even start. Even if you don't put your hands in your pockets, the sound of coins and keys jingling as you move around is annoying.

Touching your face or neck: Most of us make some gestures without realising. If possible, video yourself presenting and see if you often put your hand in front of your mouth, scratch your nose or fiddle with an earring or necklace. This can be interpreted as a sign that you have something to hide so the rule is: however much it itches, don't scratch it until later!

Hand gestures: There is a famous election picture of Margaret Thatcher in which she is making a 'V for Victory' sign with her fingers to the photographer. Unfortunately, her hand is turned the wrong way round, thus sending a completely inappropriate message to the world! The problem with hand gestures is that it's quite easy to make a cross-cultural faux pas that can ruin all your hard work. Take a 'T' sign made with both hands, for instance. In Europe and the US, it means 'time out' but in Japan, you're asking for the bill. In general, it's best to avoid hand gestures, however harmless you think they are. After all, is there anything more embarrassing than trying to high-five someone and missing?

Talking to the screen: We've already discussed how important it is to try to make as much eye contact as possible with your audience. There are times, however, when you need to turn to look at a detail on your screen, or you need a prompt to help you to get back on track after you've answered a question. This is OK but you should try to avoid talking to the screen rather than the audience. To manage this, simply follow the three-T routine.

- Think – look at the screen and think what you want to say.

- Turn – turn back and face the audience.

- Talk – tell them what you want to say.

There's nothing wrong with pausing for a few seconds while you collect your thoughts. Your audience won't notice it.

Audience body language

So far we've looked at the presenter's body language and it's very easy to focus only on that side of things. After all, we've got enough to do making sure we're standing straight, making the right amount and kind of eye contact, not fidgeting unnecessarily and moving around appropriately. But that's only half the picture. We also need to observe the audience carefully to see what clues we can pick up as we're talking, because if we spot certain signs, we can adjust our presentation and influence their behaviour.

Positive signals

The ideal audience are all sitting on the edge of their seats and listening intently. They aren't moving very much if at all and are following what you have to say. If that's what you see in front of you, well done! Carry on as before.

Negative signals

Negative feedback is actually useful because it shows you where you need to try harder. If you notice that people are sitting back, looking at their watches or out the window, checking their phones for messages or whispering something to a neighbour, their attention may be starting to flag. If that's the case, it's time to take action. So what are your options?

Taking action

1 Adjust your volume

One possible reason why your audience isn't paying close attention is that they can't hear you clearly. If it's the people at the back of the room who are getting restless, try talking louder, more slowly and more clearly and see if that makes any difference. You can also adopt the opposite tactic and lower your voice. This can have the effect of forcing people to stop fidgeting because they can't hear you otherwise.

2 Be silent

This is the extreme extension of the previous suggestion. People from Western cultures are generally uncomfortable with silence so you may find this hard to do. It is, however, very effective. Simply stop talking and stare in the direction from which the noise is coming. Don't say anything; simply wait for about fifteen seconds and peer pressure will force those who aren't paying attention to refocus. This tactic is also absolutely brilliant if somebody's mobile phone starts ringing when you're talking. The guilty party will desperately try to turn it off; just wait until they've done so and then, without commenting, carry on from where you left off. Be cool and don't show that you are in the least perturbed.

3 Ask a question

This is a good alternative to the previous option. Look in the direction of the noise and say: *Sorry, did you want to ask a question about the last point? No? OK ...* Again, it's important that you remain completely unruffled by the situation. Your audience will be impressed.

Specific negative signals

1 Restlessness

A presentation should always be a two-way process: you're giving the audience information, but if some of the information is redundant or irrelevant, they'll start to get restless. In this case, you'll probably notice signs of lack of concentration amongst people near the front as well as the back. There could be several reasons for this: the content of your presentation may be too basic for them. On the other hand, it may be too complex and detailed or you may have overloaded your visuals with information and they can't follow you any more. You need to be flexible in such cases and instead of ploughing on like the Titanic towards an iceberg, see if you can put your message another way, simplify it or highlight the key point with a laser pointer.

2 Rejection

What if you have something controversial to say? You can normally see people's opinion clearly mirrored in their body language and if somebody disagrees with what you're saying, arms and legs will probably be crossed and lips pursed. Or they'll be sitting back in their seats with one hand propping their chin looking dubious. You can, of course, simply ignore these signs and carry on – and this might be appropriate in particular circumstances. Alternatively, you can try and engage the sceptics in discussion on the topic. This takes courage but it is the best way to win them over to your opinion. Ask questions to discover what's bothering them.

- *What do you think about this point?*

- *Does that make sense to you?*

- *Would you like to comment?*

- *How do you feel about this?*

In Step 7 we'll cover techniques for handling questions in more detail but the general point to be aware of here is that the best presentations come across as a dialogue between friends. You don't have to agree with everything members of the audience say and if necessary, you may have to suggest agreeing to disagree. But if you pay your participants the compliment of listening respectfully to their opinion, your chances of success will be greatly increased.

3 Confusion

Confusion is different from rejection. You'll notice that people are looking blank, shrugging their shoulders or turning to a neighbour for an explanation. This can be demoralising but it should be exploited as an opportunity to find another way to get your message across. Here are some possibilities.

■ Summarise each key point before you move on to the next topic:
  Let me recap that last point. This software upgrade is going to …

■ Ask for feedback on each point before you move on:
  Would it be helpful if I went over the data security question again?

■ Provide an additional explanation of the problem point:
  Another reason why speed is important is that our competitors are already able to …

■ See if you can find a suitable metaphor for your topic:
  This feedback loop is similar to traffic flowing through a one-way traffic system …

It's an uncomfortable fact but if your audience hasn't understood something, it's your fault, not theirs. Your job is to get your message across to the people in your audience and your research should have helped you to design your presentation so that it was pitched at the right level. If it's not getting through, you didn't do your job properly. But if you're able to read your audience's body language, you can rescue the situation. Don't carry on regardless; engage with them and find a way to clear up whatever it is they haven't understood.

Dry-run checklist

Before you give a presentation, video yourself doing a dry run to a couple of friends and then check your performance using this checklist. Give yourself marks out of ten (0 = rubbish, 10 = brilliant). It will help you when it comes to the real thing.

Presentation aspect	Score	Comment
Appropriate appearance		
Pockets emptied of coins, keys, mobile phone, etc.		
Head and shoulders back		
Confident stance		
Eyes on the audience, not on notes		
Pointing from the shoulder		
Appropriate use of hands		
Appropriate movements in the presentation space		
Appropriate reactions to the audience		

Key take-aways

Think about the things you will take away from Step 5 and how you will implement them.

Topic	Take-away	Implementation
Understanding why non-verbal communication is important when giving presentations	• *Studies show presentation success or failure is largely influenced by the presenter's body language.*	• *Watch other presenters, e.g. news readers, politicians and actors, and note how their body language influences success or failure.*
Using facial body language to improve my presentations		
Using arm and hand movements to improve my presentations		
Using movement within the presentation space		
Avoiding bad body language habits		
Using posture to give a positive message		
Interpreting and dealing with the audience's body language		

Step 6

DEAL WITH NERVES

'There are only two types of speakers in the world: 1) the nervous and 2) liars.'
Mark Twain, US writer (1835–1910)

Five ways to succeed

■ Recognise the symptoms of nerves.

■ Recognise the positive aspects of nerves.

■ Try different relaxation and confidence-building techniques.

■ Do a dry run and collect positive feedback.

■ Make sure you eat something before your presentation.

Five ways to fail

■ Ignore the possibility of nerves before the presentation.

■ Give up the opportunity to give a presentation.

■ Think your audience is hostile.

■ Talk quickly and finish your presentation too soon.

■ Avoid looking at the audience.

The effects of nervousness

We are not alone

On the internet it's possible to find many top-ten lists of people's greatest fears. Always included in these lists is glossophobia – the fear of public speaking. Why is this? The main cause is the unfamiliarity of the situation. In a presentation we talk one-way to a group of people we often don't know and by whom we feel we're being judged. In these circumstances it's perfectly normal to feel nervous. But that doesn't have to be a bad thing. When you're nervous, your body generates adrenalin, a hormone which causes the 'fight or flight' response. This is the natural response of all animals to a threatening situation: we either run away from the threat or we stay and fight the source of the threat. Which is not really desirable in the context of giving a presentation.

However, small amounts of adrenalin make you feel more alive, quicker to react and generally a more exciting presenter for your audience. So your aim shouldn't be to deny having nerves or to attempt to ignore them; it should be to manage your nerves so that the positive effects of adrenalin will help you and the negative effects won't harm you. So what are the negative effects?

Negative effects

These vary enormously from person to person, but typically people notice one or more of these symptoms:

- complete loss of self-confidence
- cold hands
- dry mouth or throat, squeaky voice
- sweating, blushing, stress rash
- problems with breathing
- rapid heart rate
- butterflies or feelings of nausea
- blankness

All of these can obviously impede your ability to give your presentation your best shot so firstly we're going to look at a number of pre-presentation techniques that can be used to boost your overall self-confidence. Then we'll look at some simple and easy ways to deal with the physical symptoms should they appear.

Building self-confidence

It makes sense to try to eliminate any problems with nerves before your presentation and the techniques we're going to look at all work. The question is finding which ones work best for you so try them out, see which ones you like and use them whenever you give a presentation.

Being prepared for anything

Like a good boy scout or girl guide, a good presenter is always prepared for anything. The constant theme of this book has been how careful preparation can turn you into a really effective presenter. When you stand up to deliver, you should feel that you've done everything possible to prepare for a first-class presentation.

To give yourself extra confidence, it's a good idea to learn the first two minutes of your presentation by heart so that you don't need to look at any notes, cards, slides or anything except the audience. As we've already discussed in Step 2, you should *not* apply this approach to the whole presentation because you won't sound spontaneous. But learning at least the beginning by heart will help you to get over any start-up nerves and get you off to a flying start.

Visualisation

It's a curious fact that most of us tend to focus on what we do wrong rather than what we do well. This is partly due to our education system, which has conditioned us to find mistakes in our work. The problem with this mentality is that we tend to ignore the things we get right, which in turn makes us feel inadequate. Just before a presentation, this is the last thing you should be feeling.

Visualisation lists and visualisation scripts are powerful tools that help you to see the good things you've already done and also help you to focus your emotions and thoughts on the positive end result.

Visualisation lists

These are very easy to prepare. The night before your presentation, write out – preferably by hand, it's more effective – the beginning of this sentence, twenty times:

I'm a successful and well-prepared presenter because …

When you've done that, think of all the work you've put in to prepare for your presentation and complete each sentence in twenty different ways. For example:

I'm a successful and well-prepared presenter because I've done a dry run of my presentation with Tina.

I'm a successful and well-prepared presenter because I've checked the meeting room and equipment.

When you've finished, read the sentences and give yourself a pat on the back for all your hard work. Go to bed, sleep well and read them again before you set off to wherever you are giving your presentation.

Visualisation scripts

People who do a lot of sport may already be familiar with this kind of visualisation. You imagine the outcome you want and play it like a film in your head before the actual event. Wayne Rooney, for example, visualises scoring particular kinds of goals before every game. It's also been found that when a player is injured, simply visualising the exercises they'd normally do or the movements they'd normally make ensures that the muscles they need for these activities don't deteriorate as quickly as they would without the visualisation. You can apply this technique to presentations, either by describing your presentation in writing or by closing your eyes and playing it like a film in your head. A typical visualisation script could run like this:

> I'm in the presentation room, everything has been set up in advance and the technical check worked perfectly. I'm confident and excited about what's about to happen. The room is comfortable and the audience look keen and interested. I can see people I know and they smile encouragingly at me. As I start, my words flow easily, my visuals are convincing and the audience nods in agreement. They ask good questions and I answer them with authority and self-confidence. I wrap up the presentation with a powerful conclusion and they clap with real enthusiasm. At the end, several people stay behind to ask more questions and congratulate me on what I said.

The important thing is to add as much realistic detail as possible to the scenario to make it believable.

Reducing stress

As we mentioned earlier, a certain amount of adrenalin when presenting is a good thing, but too much can produce the 'fight or flight' response. Generally speaking, presenters don't fight with their audience but occasionally people do take flight and refuse to give their talk.

The problem with a stressful situation like presenting is that it generates the same adrenalin our bodies needed to run away from or fight with sabre-tooth tigers when we were cave people. Unfortunately, we don't perform the physical actions that would use it up. Consequently, the adrenalin remains in our system making us feel tense. So what can you do about it? The following techniques can be used shortly before you're due to give a presentation.

Taking a walk

A quick walk around the block is an excellent coping method. The muscle activity will reduce the adrenalin in your body and stop you feeling anxious. If walking proves difficult because of where you are, walk up and down a couple of flights of stairs. The advantage of both of these exercises is that they not only reduce the adrenalin to manageable levels, they also pump oxygen around your body so you should feel on top of your game when you begin your presentation.

Stretching

When you're presenting, you want to feel that you can move around comfortably and naturally in front of your audience. Below are two easy exercises you can do in the office to help you to get warmed up in advance. However, do be careful about trying them if you have a back problem.

Stand stretching

1 Stand straight with your legs apart and arms by your side, shoulders back and head up. Relax your face muscles and bend your legs slightly at the knee.

2 Keep your feet on the ground and slowly stretch your arms up as far as you can. Really try to reach the ceiling.

3 Let your torso flop forward so that you bend at the waist and your arms can swing between your slightly bent legs.

4 Straighten your legs slowly and then even more slowly straighten your back so that you are back to the first position again.

5 Repeat two more times.

Sit stretching

1 Sit in a good chair with your lower back pushed into the base of the chair back, shoulders back and head up, with your hands resting on your thighs and your feet flat on the ground.

2 Lift your arms as high as possible and stretch towards the ceiling. Really try and touch it with your fingers.

3 Lower your arms, bend forwards, stretch out your legs and try to touch your toes.

4 Sit back up straight again.

5 Repeat two more times.

Clearing the brain

This exercise sounds contradictory. Just before a presentation you probably feel that you should be concentrating on all the things you have to do. (PowerPoint on? Check! Notes organised? Check! Mobile off? Check!) In fact, it's helpful to clear your brain of everything just before your presentation as this reduces the risk of a last-minute panic, which generates a lot of adrenalin. If you've done all your preparation work, you've already got everything organised so the technique described below allows you to start your presentation with a clean slate.

1 Sit in a chair with your feet flat on the floor, your back straight and your hands resting on your thighs.

2 Close your eyes or fix them on a point on the wall in front of you.

3 Breathe in deeply through your nose. Hold your breath for two seconds and then breathe out through your mouth. Allow your body to tilt back slightly as you breathe out.

4 Repeat three times.

5 Now repeat the exercise, but this time, when you breathe in, say to yourself *Empty mind*! On the out-breath, say *Nothing*!

6 Carry on with this exercise for as long as you want.

The first time you try this, you might want to do it when you're alone. But with practice you can actually do it very discreetly so that nobody notices, even when you're travelling on public transport. Just make sure you don't start staring blankly at somebody's face. They might take exception.

Power poses

In Step 5 we looked at how your body language can have an impact on your audience. Now we're going to see how you can use your own body language to influence your own self-confidence. Read the situations below.

Situation 1: If you were an actor in a film and you wanted to show the bad guys that you weren't afraid, what position would you take? Maybe you'd stand with your feet apart, hands on your hips, with your shoulders back and head up, looking powerful. Like Wonder Woman or Superman.

Situation 2: Now imagine you're a guilty suspect who's being interviewed by the police in a prison cell. How would you sit? Perhaps you'd have your legs and arms crossed in front of your body as if to prevent yourself giving anything away.

Situation 3: Finally, imagine you're an athlete who's just won a gold medal at the Olympics. You're standing in front of thousands of fans and they're cheering and clapping. How do you react? Probably you raise both arms above your head in a victory salute.

Now here comes the interesting part. If these were real situations, you would find that in 1 and 3 the protagonists had relatively high levels of the hormone testosterone and low levels of the hormone cortisol, while in situation 2 the guilty suspect would have high cortisol and low testosterone. Our bodies generate testosterone when we feel powerful and cortisol when we feel weak and defensive.

OK, now here comes the weird part. Even if you were only acting these roles, you would generate different levels of testosterone and cortisol, depending on the poses you took. This means that just by adopting the poses described in situations 1 and 3 you can give yourself a shot of confidence-boosting testosterone. This phenomenon was discovered by Dr Amy Cuddy, a social psychologist and researcher at Harvard Business School, who was looking for ways to encourage her female students to participate more actively in the seminars that she ran. Now obviously, it would be impractical and exhausting for students or presenters to stand around in seminars or presentations with their hands permanently above their heads or on their hips so how can we make use of this information?

Dr Cuddy tested her hypothesis on her students. What she found was that adopting a power pose and holding it for a couple of minutes in advance of a stressful task helped the individual to cope much better with the task and to get the results that they wanted. Conversely, if the individual sat slumped in a chair with their head down and their arms and legs crossed protectively in front of their body, their results were worse. So here's how you could apply this knowledge to your own presentation.

1 Shortly before you have to go to your presentation venue, find a place where you'll be undisturbed or lock yourself in a stall in a lavatory.

2 Select one of the two poses (Wonder Woman or 'Victory') and stand in this pose for two minutes. You could also use this time to run the visualisation script in your head.

3 Just before your presentation, make sure you aren't sitting in a defensive position. Sit up, look ahead and radiate the confidence you feel.

In print this all sounds a bit implausible but as we have already discussed, our body language has a direct effect on the way other people perceive us so why shouldn't it also have a physiological effect on ourselves? And the raised levels of testosterone and reduced levels of cortisol that Dr Cuddy discovered show that something interesting was definitely going on with her students. So why not give it a shot and see what happens?

Last-minute symptoms

So far we've looked at the steps you can take before your presentation to reduce overall levels of stress and boost your self-confidence. But what can you do about those last-minute symptoms we listed on page 107? Here are some really easy practical tips for coping with them.

Cold hands

One clear physiological symptom of stress is when your fingers and hands go cold. This is because your body is diverting blood from your extremities to make sure that it has enough blood and oxygen for your essential organs as part of the 'fight or flight' response we looked at earlier. As soon as you become aware of this sensation, your feelings of tension intensify and a vicious cycle begins, causing stress levels to spiral.

An easy way to deal with cold hands and fingers is to get yourself a warm drink and hold it so that your hands warm up. This has an additional benefit: your subconscious registers that your fingers are no longer cold, concludes that the situation is no longer dangerous and it allows you to relax. So a cup of coffee is the answer. Right? Wrong! We'll see why in the next tip.

Dry mouth or throat

This is one of the most irritating and perverse symptoms of stress when we are presenting. Exactly when we want our voice to be as clear and as well-modulated as that of Stephen Fry or Helen Mirren, adrenalin makes us squeak like a Disney cartoon character.

The answer, of course, is liquid and the easiest solution would appear to be coffee. Unfortunately, unless the coffee is decaffeinated, this isn't a good idea. You really don't need to have any stimulants added to the adrenalin that is already charging round your system and causing your throat to seize up in the first place. For the same reason, you should steer clear of soda or energy drinks; they'll simply make you as hyperactive as a five-year-old at a birthday party.

The best solution is the most boring: have a cup of warm water, and if that's not possible, herbal tea. It's sensible to avoid warm milky drinks such as hot chocolate as they generate mucus, which can clog your vocal chords. There's nothing less attractive than a presenter clearing a frog in their throat over a loudspeaker system.

Finally, make sure that you have a glass of water near you during the presentation itself. You probably won't need it if you've had some warm water just before but it's reassuring to know it's there if you do.

Sweating, blushing, stress rash

Instead of cold hands, adrenalin can cause some people to have the opposite reaction to a stressful situation: they sweat more than usual. The result can be a presenter standing in front of an audience with dark rings under their arms, mopping their face and radiating panic signals. If this could happen to you, here are some steps you can take to avoid it being a problem.

■ **Anti-perspirant:** Don't forget it before you get dressed.

■ **Clothes:** Wear a short-sleeved cotton T-shirt next to your skin. This will absorb most of any sweat that you produce and stop it reaching the outer layers. On top you should wear a white or black blouse or shirt. Don't wear blue or red as they will show clear sweat rings should it soak through your T-shirt. Carry a cotton handkerchief (clean!) so that if you need to wipe your face or hands, you can do so easily. A handkerchief is better than a tissue; damp tissue can leave behind shreds on your nose or chin.

■ **Arrival time:** Be at the venue about fifteen minutes beforehand so you have time to relax.

■ **Blushing and stress rash:** This is a purely short-term physiological reaction to stress when you begin your talk. Concentrate on your presentation and the rash will fade. Women who are affected by a stress rash tend to get it on their neck. If this happens to you, simply wear a scarf or a high-necked blouse for the duration of the presentation.

Problems with breathing

If you are very tense before you begin speaking, you might find that your chest feels constricted and you're short of breath. This is usually due to adrenalin, which causes the muscles in your chest to tighten to protect your heart and lungs. Before getting up to speak, take the time to breathe from your diaphragm. Put your hand on your belly so you can feel it move and breathe in deeply through your nose, expelling the air through your mouth. Repeat this several times. This will relieve your symptoms. Any time you feel the problem recurring, you can simply repeat the action.

Rapid heart rate

When you're nervous, your heart beats faster to pump more blood around your body so that your muscles are ready for physical action. To slow down your heart rate, combine controlled breathing with a conscious effort to do everything more deliberately. Look around the audience to see who is there. Talk more slowly and with a more deliberate articulation. Give the audience time to absorb your visuals. Move slowly from one position to another. Calmly pick up your glass of water to have a sip. Put it down carefully. Don't talk while you're doing these actions. Your subconscious will decide that if you're being so cool, you must be unstressed, and your heart rate will slow.

These sensations can be unpleasant. The important thing to realise, however, is that by deliberately controlling your breathing and your actions, you can control the symptoms.

Nausea and butterflies

Many people don't appreciate the risk of trying to do something stressful on a completely empty stomach. The gut has an enormous number of nerve endings and if they have nothing to do because there's no food in your stomach, they'll react to your stress and emotion, giving you the feeling of butterflies. Furthermore, there's a danger that you'll feel dizzy or even faint as the situation overwhelms you.

So ignore the adrenalin which says you don't want anything inside you that might slow you down and eat something small like a yoghurt or a banana, which are easy to absorb and give you energy quickly and easily without making you feel heavy.

Blankness

Sometimes, a nervous speaker stands in front of an audience and goes blank; suddenly they can't think of what they're supposed to be saying. In Western cultures we tend to respond quickly when told to start talking. But the truth is, we don't have to. We can give ourselves a moment to relax and remind ourselves of what we want to say before we open our mouths. Here are some steps to help you if you go blank.

1 Realise that this state is temporary and it will pass in a moment.

2 Do the deep breathing exercise to allow more oxygen to reach your brain.

3 Have a sip of water.

4 Look at your notes (if you've made yourself some cards) in order to remind yourself how you want to start.

5 Look at the presentation slides on the computer screen if you have no notes.

6 Look out at the audience again, smile and then start your presentation.

The important point to remember is that what feels like an eternity to you will probably not last more than five to ten seconds. Then you'll be back on track again. Five to ten seconds is no problem for an audience. To them, it will probably just be time to make themselves comfortable and settle down before you start. And even if they notice your hesitation, so what? They'll forget it the moment you begin.

Give yourself a break

After all this emphasis on how to handle nerves, it's important to put everything into perspective. Yes, it is important to come across well when you give a presentation but don't blow things out of all proportion. Woody Allen once said: *Eighty per cent of success is just showing up.* And it's very important to remember this. As far as the audience is concerned, you've already fulfilled most of their requirements by being there at all.

Better still, your audience mostly doesn't even notice if you're nervous or not and this has been scientifically proven. In experiments carried out in 1998 and 2003, two social psychologists, Thomas Gilovitch and Kenneth Savitsky, asked both presenters and their audience to rate how nervous the presenters appeared. The presenters consistently rated themselves as appearing much more nervous than the audience did. You may feel it's obvious to everybody that you're a nervous wreck but it really isn't. To your audience, you probably look as cool as a cucumber.

So always remember: the audience can't actually see how you feel inside. And the more experience you have of presentations, the more you'll see yourself as the audience sees you.

Key take-aways

Think about the things you will take away from Step 6 and how you will implement them.

Topic	Take-away	Implementation
Recognising the positive aspects of presentation nerves	• *Adrenalin in small doses aids performance.*	• *Observe how I react in stressful situations.*
Recognising the negative aspects of presentation nerves		
How to increase my confidence before a presentation		
How to reduce stress before a presentation		
How to deal with cold hands		
How to deal with a dry mouth, throat or squeaky voice		
How to deal with sweating, blushing or stress rash		
How to deal with shallow breathing and rapid heart rate		
How to deal with butterflies and feelings of nausea		
How to keep presentation nerves in perspective		

Step 7

TURN QUESTIONS TO YOUR ADVANTAGE

'Sometimes in public life, people ask inappropriate off-the-wall kinds of question, don't they?'
— Hillary Clinton, US politician

Five ways to succeed

■ View questions positively.

■ Prepare in advance for possible question topics.

■ Listen carefully and check comprehension before answering.

■ Accept input from members of the audience.

■ Get back to people if you can't answer straightaway.

Five ways to fail

■ Refuse to take questions.

■ Allow a questioner to dominate the presentation.

■ Pretend you have an answer when you don't.

■ Only take 'friendly' questions.

■ React aggressively to difficult questions.

The benefits of questions

Sometimes presenters regard questions from the audience as a necessary evil: they have to answer them but they'd much rather not. They worry that the questions will be unpredictable and they worry that they won't have the answers. This is a mistake. Most of the time, questions are a compliment from the audience; they show they're interested in your topic and want to know more. Furthermore, questions provide an opportunity for you to check which areas are important to the audience so that you can expand on them and provide more information or clear up misunderstandings.

But what about you asking the *audience* questions? If you're giving neutral information such as delivery details or a time schedule, this might not be appropriate. In fact, asking the audience questions in this type of situation could sound very teacherly, which should be avoided. However, when you need to motivate or persuade, asking the audience questions can make your presentation more interactive so that the barrier between you and them is removed. These questions are different from the rhetorical questions we looked at in Step 4 (which don't require an answer) because they turn the presentation into a dialogue between equals rather than a monologue.

Handling questions

First let's look at some techniques for handling questions confidently. These ideas can be used in meetings or in a sales conversation with a prospective client as well as in your presentations. In fact, they can be applied to a wide range of situations.

Compliment the questioner

A bit of flattery will get you very far. It's a sad feature of business life that we rarely get positive feedback from the people around us. This is not to say you should be a phoney and go over the top with flattery but when somebody asks you a question that stretches you or gives you the opportunity to talk about an important aspect of your topic, let them know you think it's a good question.

Paraphrase the question

This is useful for several reasons. Firstly, the questioner feels that you're listening carefully and taking them seriously. Secondly, it ensures that you really have understood what the question is about. Thirdly, it gives you an opportunity to think of a response. This is especially useful in situations where you aren't sure of the answer.

Ask for a repetition

Paraphrasing isn't always possible. If you couldn't hear the question or if the questioner has a strong accent, you need to ask for a repetition: *I'm very sorry, I couldn't quite hear you. Could you repeat the question for me, please*? There's nothing wrong with doing this and it's better than pretending you've understood what was asked. After the repetition, try to repeat the question word for word so that the rest of the audience (who probably also had difficulties) also understand the question.

Ask for clarification

It's not always clear what is meant by a particular question and even after the questioner has repeated it, you may still be none the wiser. It's embarrassing to then try and give a lengthy answer and to ask if the answer was helpful only to be told, no. This is a difficult situation to be in so it's better to be up-front and honest rather than trying to bluff. Try saying: *Unfortunately, I haven't quite understood your question. Could you put it another way for me, please?*

Speculate

If you're unsure about the answer to a question but you have a rough idea, then it's perfectly legitimate to speculate as long as you make it clear that this is what you're doing. You can do this by using phrases like the ones highlighted below.

Q: *How many additional experts would be needed for the project?*

A: *That's a difficult question.* **I think it's possible that** *we'll only need four or five* **if we can** *also use some of our current staff. But* **it may be necessary to** *double that number if our own people are working on other projects.*

Speculating is useful because you're not committing yourself to anything and you've left the door open for other possibilities. Just make sure you don't overdo it, though. You should only speculate when necessary; otherwise you'll give your audience the feeling that it's impossible to get a concrete answer out of you.

Pass the question

You yourself may not know the answer to a particular question but if you're sharing the presentation, your partner might be able to deal with it. Don't feel that you have to be responsible for all the answers; pass the question to somebody else if it makes sense. For example:

Q: *How much does data storage cost?*

A: *Hm, that's an interesting question. Can I hand you over to my colleague, Ben, who is our data storage specialist?*

If somebody in the audience volunteers the answer, make sure you're gracious and thank them for their help.

Always tell the truth

It's more than likely that at some stage, somebody will ask you a question to which you don't know the answer, however carefully you've prepared. Simply apologise, say you don't know the answer, offer to find out after the presentation and promise to get back to them as soon as possible. And don't forget to keep your promise! For example:

Q: What kind of training will the new staff need?

A: I'm very sorry but unfortunately, I don't have that information at the moment. The program is still in development. As soon as it's ready, I'll provide that information.

So why isn't it a good idea to try and bluff and simply pretend you know the answer? Firstly, you can be sure that the moment you do, some person in the audience will put up their hand and contradict you. This is likely to be extremely embarrassing for you. If you realise that the person is right, you can apologise and claim your bluff was a genuine mistake but even so, you still end up with egg on your face. Alternatively, you might feel you have to defend your original statement and start an argument about who's right, which is embarrassing for everybody. Secondly, there's nothing wrong with not being all-knowing. Far better to admit to a gap in your knowledge and then rectify it than send people away with incorrect information that could well come back to haunt you at a later time.

Cross-cultural considerations

It's important to be aware that there are strong cultural and language considerations when it comes to asking and answering questions. In the West, the education system is based on the teacher and student engaging in questions and answers. In parts of Asia influenced by Confucian thinking, students are expected to listen rather than question. In fact, questions can be seen as showing disrespect to the presenter: they imply that the explanation provided the first time round wasn't good enough, which could cause the presenter to lose face. This means that if you're giving a talk to a group of people from Korea or Japan, you need to consider that there may be not only a language barrier but also a cultural one to asking questions, which is considerably greater than that facing a person from a Western culture.

The result can be that while you are giving your presentation, you get the feeling that there is no buy-in from the audience because they're reluctant to open their mouths. This reluctance isn't confined to people from Asia, of course. There are many reasons why an audience might be quiet but it's a shame because they might be missing an opportunity to have something useful clarified for them.

But is it the responsibility of the presenter to drag questions out of the audience by hook or by crook? Ultimately, no. You're responsible for the content and delivery of your presentation and the audience is responsible for making the best use of this opportunity. However, a simple technique that you can use with any audience that seems a little reticent about asking questions is to get them to prepare questions in pairs or small groups.

1 Warn the audience in advance that at a particular stage in the presentation you would like to take their questions. It could be at the end, it could be after you've explained an important point.

2 When you've reached the pre-defined point, tell them they have two to three minutes to discuss with their neighbour any questions they'd like you to answer. Observe which pairs seem to be engaged in discussion.

3 After a few minutes, ask what questions they've come up with, focusing initially on pairs who seemed to have been talking to each other.

This approach is effective because it's more comfortable for some people to share responsibility for asking a question.

Finally, a word of warning: don't go into your presentation with preconceptions about how the audience will react. You could be presenting to a group of Taiwanese businesspeople who've all studied in the US and are more than happy to bombard you with questions. Use your observation skills and always adjust your behaviour to the people in front of you.

Preparing for questions

Although the quote from Hillary Clinton on page 125 is accurate, and occasionally you can be asked something completely unpredictable, it's generally possible to anticipate most questions. So, as with all other aspects of presenting, preparation is the key to dealing with questions successfully. There are two things you can do.

■ Do a dry run of your presentation with a friend as your audience and encourage them to ask as many questions as they can. If possible, video yourself and think about what questions you would ask.

■ Examine each slide carefully and try to think of every possible question that somebody could ask about it.

Look at the example slide below. What questions could you ask about it?

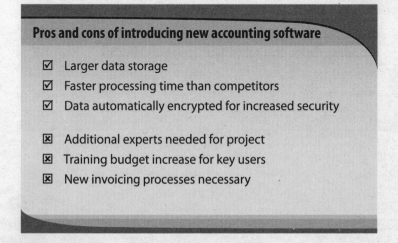

Pros and cons of introducing new accounting software

☑ Larger data storage
☑ Faster processing time than competitors
☑ Data automatically encrypted for increased security

☒ Additional experts needed for project
☒ Training budget increase for key users
☒ New invoicing processes necessary

Here are some possible questions that you could expect.

- How much data do we currently store?

- Have you tested competitors' software or are you relying on information from the provider of the new software?

- Have you measured the increased speed?

- Do we need to encrypt our data?

- Will encrypting slow the user experience?

- What computer language is the new software based on?

- Why do you think we need additional experts for this project?

- Why would the key users need additional training?

- Who would provide the training?

- What kind of training would they need?

- Do you know who the key users are?

- Why would the invoice processes need to be changed?

The point is not that you're likely to be asked all of these questions; the point is that if you've thought through the possibilities in advance and know what to say, you'll feel relaxed and confident about dealing with them if they do arise.

Question types

An audience is made up of people with different interests and reasons for attending a presentation. Some people will be there because they really need the information that you're going to present. Other will be there because their boss has asked them to come but they themselves don't really have any interest in the topic. Yet others may just want to raise their profile in the company by showing interest or asking critical questions. This means that a person who asks a question isn't necessarily just asking for information. In this section, we'll analyse some of the different types of questions that audience members ask and how you can deal with them most effectively.

Information-checking questions

To deal with this common type of question, follow these steps.

- Thank the person for their question and compliment them on asking it.

- Answer the question, preferably with a concrete example that the audience can relate to.

- Check that they've understood. For example:

   Q: *How much data do we currently store?*
   A: *Thank you, that's an important point. Our system can handle up to 100,000 invoices every day. That's four invoices every second of an eight-hour working day, which is a lot of data.*
   Q: *Right.*
   A: *Does that help?*

Misunderstandings

If it's clear from the question that somebody has misunderstood a point, you have to take the blame, however ridiculous the misunderstanding. Don't cause the questioner to lose face.

- Paraphrase the question to check you're talking about the same point.

- Go back to a relevant visual aid if you have one or repeat the point you made previously – but slowly and clearly.

- Check that the person has understood the issue. You can apologise if you feel it's appropriate. For example:

   Q: *Do we need to store this data?*
   A: *You'd like to know why we store the data – is that right?*
   Q: *Yes.*
   A: *OK. If you look at this slide … You can see that we need it for audit purposes. Is that clearer?*
   Q: *I see.*
   A: *Sorry, I should have emphasised that more clearly.*

Irrelevant questions

It is possible that somebody will ask something off topic. Again, try not to cause them to lose face but move on quickly.

■ Paraphrase the question to check you've understood.

■ Explain why the point doesn't apply to this presentation and, if possible, where they can get the information they want.

■ Continue the presentation or deal with the next question. For example:

Q: Why do we have audits?

A: So what you're asking is: what is the purpose of having audits? Have I understood you correctly?

Q: Yes.

A: Unfortunately, that's beyond the scope of my presentation. Perhaps you can discuss that with the accounts department.

Q: I see.

A: Can I have the next question, please?

Technical questions

It is possible that somebody will ask for a lot of technical information that isn't of any interest to the audience.

■ Compliment the questioner.

■ Explain why you can't answer the question now.

■ Offer to explain to them after the presentation. For example:

Q: What computer language is the new software based on? ABAP or Java?

A: That's a tough question and I'd prefer not to focus on the technical details here. Would you have time after my presentation so we could discuss this together?

Political questions

All companies have people who are more interested in politics than business. Sometimes you could be making a suggestion that has an impact on an individual's position or work. These situations have to be handled delicately. Take a question like this:

Why do you think we need additional experts for this project?

This could be a simple request for information but there could be a subtext implicit if the person asking the question is head of the IT department. They might see the recommendation as a criticism of their current team. Your best course of action is to make sure you've prepared good supporting arguments for any presentation points that might be controversial and avoid a political discussion in front of an audience by offering to discuss the matter with the person later.

■ Compliment the questioner.

■ Explain why you don't want to answer the question now.

■ Offer to discuss the matter with them after the presentation. For example:

Q: *Why do you think we need additional experts for this project?*

A: *That's an important question but I think you and I should look at the reasons together. Would you have time after my presentation so we could discuss them?*

Alternatively, you can make sure that you've talked through any controversial matters in advance with people likely to be affected by your proposals. That way they won't feel ambushed by the content of your presentation.

Asking the audience questions

At the beginning of this step, we discussed the usefulness of asking the audience questions, particularly if we need to motivate or persuade them to take our recommended course of action. Of course, that's not the only reason for asking your audience questions. One of the interesting things about the development of online presentations is that the internet platforms used include a number of tools allowing the presenter to get a reaction from the audience as they go along. These mostly take the form of small multiple-choice questionnaires or *yes/no* questions and they're helpful in keeping the audience involved and allowing the presenter to see if the content is relevant. But their purpose isn't to get the audience excited or enthusiastic about the topic. In this section, we're going to look at how, in a face-to-face situation, you can pose the kind of questions that help you to get your message across more powerfully. Here are some basic do's and don't's.

Do:

■ Be clear and concise.

■ Use your question to focus on one point only.

■ Spread your questions around the audience.

Don't:

■ Ask more than one question per presentation point.

■ Ask questions the audience can't answer.

Question types

In general, it's a good idea to try to use open questions (e.g. *what? where? why? how?*) rather than *yes/no* questions. Your questions should be thought-provoking and stimulating and call on the audience's experience and elicit their views and opinions. Try and start with phrases like the following.

- *What's your view on …?*

- *How do you feel about …?*

- *What would you do if …?*

- *What might be the best way to …?*

Of course, it's important that you yourself have an opinion about the topic that you're referring to but don't be dogmatic if you're going to involve the audience in this way. They're entitled to their point of view even if it differs from yours.

Here are some different question types you can try.

1 Kick-off questions

These are a nice way to get the audience involved from the word go. They aren't directed at an individual but at the whole group: *Ultimately, the business of business is to make ... what?* Shrug your shoulders and look quizzically at the audience to show you would like an answer.

2 Target questions

These are useful for calling on a particular individual who you know has the relevant expertise. Establish eye contact with the person, call out their name and pose the question: *Ben, how would you describe the security of our accounting software at the moment?* However, make sure that Ben can answer the question and that he won't object to being involved in this way.

3 Delayed fuse questions

This type of question should be directed at the entire audience. Ask the question, pause and scan the room with your eyes. As the tension mounts, it should be clear to you if somebody has an answer because they'll establish eye contact. When you've found your person, pause for a second longer and then indicate them with your hand and invite them to answer: *So, in your opinion, what do you think we should be looking for with our new software provider?* (pause up to five seconds) Yes ... *The lady in the pink blouse?* This is the most stimulating form of question to ask because everybody in the audience is forced to think of an answer while you decide who to pick.

Keep control and enjoy yourself!

As the presenter, it's important to remain in control of the question and answer process. To accomplish this, there are several tools at your disposal. Firstly, you can tell the audience at the beginning if you're willing to answer questions as they occur to them or whether you'd prefer them to wait until the end of your presentation. Generally speaking, it's advisable to take questions as you go along because otherwise they can get forgotten. But if you're short of time the second approach is quite legitimate as it prevents distractions.

Secondly, you can control who gets to ask a question by indicating whose turn is next. For example, if several people ask questions at the same time, you can show them who's in charge by selecting the next questioner.

Thirdly, you can (politely) interrupt a questioner if they're talking too much:

Q: *... and what I haven't seen yet is a complete overview of the costs. I mean are we going to be ...*

A: *Sorry, can I just interrupt you there a second. Have I understood correctly? You want a cost analysis, right?*

Q: *Um ... yes.*

A: *OK. Look at slide 7 and there you can see the figures you want.*

You must never be rude but you can be firm – and that's what your audience expects of you.

Finally, remember that the question phase of the presentation is when you can be at your most spontaneous. Show your audience your enthusiasm. The applause will soon follow!

Sounding Pro

So what might you say during your presentation? Here are some options that will work in most situations:

Thanking somebody for asking a question	*Thank you, that's a good/interesting/tough/demanding/important question.*
Paraphrasing a question	*You'd like to know … Is that right/correct? / So, what you're asking is … / Correct me if I'm wrong, but you're asking … / Have I understood you right? You'd like to know if …*
Asking for clarification	*I'm very sorry, but I'm not sure I understand the question. Could you put it another way for me? / Sorry, but what exactly do you mean?*
Dealing with an irrelevant question	*Unfortunately, that's beyond the scope of my presentation. / I'm afraid that's not really the topic of the talk today.*
Deferring answering a question until later	*Would you like to discuss that question with me after my presentation? / Do you have time to talk to me later about this?*
Asking for repetition	*I didn't catch that. Could you repeat the question, please? / I'm sorry, I couldn't hear you. What was your question?*
Speculating	*It might be necessary to … / One possibility might be to … /*
Handing over questions	*I'd like to pass that question over to my colleague, Ben. / Ben, would you like to answer that question for me?*

Key take-aways

Think about the things you will take away from Step 7 and how you will implement them.

Topic	Take-away	Implementation
How to prepare for audience questions in advance	• *Try to anticipate questions.*	• *Ask a friend or colleague to watch a dry run and ask questions.* • *List all possible questions related to each slide.*
Handling questions in general		
How to handle information-checking questions		
How to handle questions from people who have misunderstood		
How to handle irrelevant questions		
How to handle technical questions		
How to handle political questions		
How to handle cross-cultural aspects of Q&A sessions		
How to ask the audience questions		
How to keep control of Q&A sessions		